P9-BZE-878

What readers are saying about
Her Name Is Woman

It's so good to know that women are special in God's eyes and that He clearly uses them for His plan on earth. We study *Her Name is Woman* every week in our Bible study group with great interest . . . .

Her Name Is Woman is such a good way to study characters from the Bible. So many times in church we hear preaching on a theme or subject but not so much on real people who struggled in life seeking God. . . . If we can put ourselves in the situation the whole story comes alive. That is what happened to us through this book.

My roomates at the university didn't know much about the Bible but they became quite interested through my reading of *Her Name Is Woman*. Each evening I would read about one new woman. God worked to allow me to explain the gospel to my roomates clearly and naturallly. Praise God!

It was good to read about women of strong character from the Bible. Many of them were humble and yet used greatly by God.

①

BOOK ONE / 24 WOMEN OF THE BIBLE

HER NAME IS WOMAN

Gien Karssen

NAVPRESS

BRINGING TRUTH TO LIFE
NavPress Publishing Group
P.O. Box 35001, Colorado Springs, Colorado 80935

◢

OUR GUARANTEE TO YOU

We believe so strongly in the message of our books that we are making this quality guarantee to you. If for any reason you are disappointed with the content of this book, return the title page to us with your name and address and we will refund to you the list price of the book. To help us serve you better, please briefly describe why you were disappointed. Mail your refund request to: NavPress, P.O. Box 35002, Colorado Springs, CO 80935.

The Navigators is an international Christian organization. Our mission is to reach, disciple, and epuip people to know Christ and to make Him known through successive generations. We envision multitudes of diverse people in the United States and every other nation who have a passionate love for Christ, live a lifestyle of sharing Christ's love, and multiply spiritual laborers among those without Christ.

NavPress is the publishing ministry of The Navigators. NavPress publications help believers learn biblical truth and apply what they learn to their livers and ministries. Our mission is to stimulate spiritual formation among our readers.

English translation © 1975 by The Navigators
All rights reserved. No part of this publication may be reproduced in any form without written permission from NavPress, P. O. Box 35001, Colorado Springs, CO 80935.
Library of Congress Catalog Card No. 77-081186
ISBN 08910-94202

(Originally published in the Netherlands as *Manninne—Vrouwen in de Bijbel*, © Buijten & Schipperheijn, Amsterdam, 1974. ISBN: 90-6064-110-8)

Editor: Monte C. Unger

Unless otherwise indicated, Scripture quotations are from the *New American Standard Bible* (NASB), © The Lockman Foundation 1960, 1962, 1963, 1968, 1971, 1972, 1973, 1975, 1977. Used by permission.

Printed in the United States of America

43 44 45 46 47 / 05 04 03 02

FOR A FREE CATALOG OF
NAVPRESS BOOKS & BIBLE STUDIES,
CALL 1-800-366-7788 (USA)
or 1-416-499-4615 (CANADA)

Dedication

I dedicate this book to my many friends within The Navigators organization around the world. The plan to write this book began to ripen through my global contact with young women. I saw in them the same fascination for the lives of women in the Bible that I have.

I also am thankful for the members of many Bible study groups in The Netherlands who checked the Bible study questions at the end of each chapter for me.

I further remember many, many others, men and women, who through their teachings, example and friendship have made an indelible impression upon my life. I think of the first Navigator I met years ago, Dawson Trotman, the founder of the organization, and of the many young people who have found a personal faith in Jesus Christ through the ministry of The Navigators recently.

They all have three things in common: a great love for God, a deep reverence for His Word and a passion to share their lives with others. Two words are applicable to almost all of them: realism and enthusiasm.

Through my fellowship with The Navigators the intense desire to be a woman after the heart of God grew within me. For this reason Eve, Sarah and others in this book are not just people of a dim, distant past, but real people, living and sparkling. It is my desire that every Navigator who reads this book, and all my other friends, will be challenged in the same way to live wholeheartedly for God. It is my desire that they be encouraged and built up. And, at the same time, I trust the book will prove to be an instrument in their hands whereby they can help others.

With this prayer I send HER NAME IS WOMAN into the world.

Gien Karssen

Contents

New Testament

Gien Karssen is a storyteller. Although there are many studies about the women in the Bible, I have never read one more practical than HER NAME IS WOMAN. Gien makes these biblical women really come alive as you observe their actions and the effects of their lives. She helps you draw out applications which are relevant today. For those who are interested in discovering more about each woman, she provides discussion questions at the end of every chapter.

Gien is one of the best trainers I know for young Bible study leaders. She brings the Word of God to bear upon situations in day-to-day living.

My prayer is that this book will work as a seed that brings forth much fruit.

Corrie ten Boom

HER NAME IS WOMAN
"Women in the Bible"

Eve. The first woman. Equal to man, she differed from him only
sexually. Though much has been written about her, the subject has
not yet been exhausted. She is the mother of all women.

The women in this book are not fictional. They are real. They
lived in history and, in their desires and problems, in their hopes
and ambitions, are living among us today. I trust that while you
read about them, they will fascinate as well as warn you. This
happened to me as I was writing about them.

The great difference between the women in this book is not
status. It doesn't matter that one is rich as the Queen of Sheba or
poor as the widow in Jesus' days, whether one is a leader like
Miriam or in disrespect like the Samaritan woman, whether one is
single or married. Those incidentals are unimportant. The real
difference between these daughters of Eve is whether or not they
know God. The central question as you learn about each of them
is, What place does God have in her life? The answer to this
question decides each one's happiness and usefulness. This is the
motivation which keeps her moving forward.

The women in this book were chosen on this basis. You will
discover that independent of age, social status or occupation, there

is one thing they all must face—their attitude toward God.

If He is given the right place in life, then one becomes attractive in a special and useful way. When He is absent, or if He is not given His rightful place, then life is without true purpose—without perspective.

I hope that you will also discover what a unique book the Bible is and, that while getting acquainted with these women, you will make a fresh or renewed start in getting to know the Word of God.

Special note: *Please read the Bible portions at the beginning of each chapter. They are necessary for understanding the chapter.*

For those who not only desire to read about the women, but also want to study their lives, either personally or in a group, there are Bible study questions at the end of each chapter. The next section contains suggestions on how to use this book for personal and group study.

Suggestions

I feel, as many do, that the most fruitful discussion results when small groups of people share what the Bible has said to them personally.

The following suggestions will be helpful for those interested in being in or in leading a Bible study group.

SUGGESTIONS FOR BIBLE STUDY GROUPS

1. Start with a small group—usually with a minimum of six and a maximum of ten people. This way your group will be large enough for an interesting discussion, but small enough for each member to participate. As your number increases, start a second group.

2. Before you start the group you should decide how often you want to meet. Many people may hesitate to give themselves to something new for an indefinite period of time. This problem can be settled if you decide beforehand to meet, for example, four to six times. If after that time period you decide to continue on, then agree on a number of meetings.

3. Remember that a Bible study group should discuss the Bible. To prevent some from riding hobby horses it is advisable that each participant prepare her study at home beforehand. Then the

meeting can be used for discussing each person's prepared study. Groups flourish where each member shares her personal findings.

4. Stress the need of applying the lessons learned, and help one another in doing this. There is a far greater need for spiritual growth than for an increase of knowledge *per se*. How can what I learned influence my life? is a question each participant should ask herself and answer during each discussion.

5. Determine, before you start, to attend every meeting. Miss only when you absolutely cannot attend. If you can't attend, do the study anyhow and make up for it at the next meeting.

6. Consider yourself a member of the group. Feel free to make a contribution. Lack of experience should not keep you from taking part in the discussion. On the other hand, resist the temptation to dominate the group.

SUGGESTIONS FOR LEADERS OF BIBLE STUDY GROUPS

1. Be sure you have given sufficient time to your own Bible study and that you have completed it.

2. Come prepared. Make notes of the points you want to stress. Approach these points with questions.

3. Teach by asking questions instead of by making statements. Few mountain climbers enjoy being carried to the top. Leave the joy of climbing to them. Don't do all the talking. Guide the discussion in such a way that each member of the group can participate.

4. Prepare thought-provoking questions. Ask questions which apply the Bible to daily life problems. Omit questions which can be answered by a simple yes or no.

5. Arrange your time and seating arrangement beforehand. (A circle is generally the best.) Begin and end on time. Unobtrusively keep your eye on your watch.

6. Pray for yourself and for each member of the group. Pray that Christ will speak to each person present by His Word. Pray that the Holy Spirit will make you sensitive to the needs of others.

Prayer results in enthusiasm, and this is absolutely essential for the success of your discussion.

These suggestions are not limited to a certain type of Bible study group. You can use the same principles for the study of Bible books, chapters or biblical subjects. Those who desire practical guidelines for Bible study should obtain *The Navigator Bible Studies Handbook.*

SUGGESTIONS FOR A GROUP DISCUSSION ABOUT EVE (an example for all the women)

1. Be sure that every member of the group has completed her own study. Encourage each to take notes during the discussion.

2. Decide ahead of time that you as a group will restrict yourselves to answering only the given Bible study questions or closely related subjects.

3. Let every discussion center around the Bible. Always ask, "What does the Bible say about this subject?"

4. The success of each Bible group discussion is strongly dependent on the questions the leader asks and on how she starts and guides the conversation. Four types of questions are:

   a. Questions to start the discussion.

   b. Questions to guide the discussion.

   c. Questions that help clarify and deepen the subject.

   d. Questions which stimulate application.

5. Examples of the above questions as pertaining to Eve:

   a. Questions to start the discussion:

      (1) What did we learn about Eve?

      (2) What did we learn about the serpent?

      (3) What did we learn about temptation?

      (4) What did we learn about the results of sin?

When you introduce every main point of the study this way, you will avoid getting the stated Bible study questions parroted back and you will guarantee an interesting discussion. It is wise to summarize one point before going on to the next.

b. Questions to guide the discussion:

(1) What did someone else discover?

(2) Does anyone else have anything to add?

(3) Is there anyone else who wishes to say something?

Address the whole group with these sorts of questions, not just one person in particular. This provides an open discussion in which everyone present can participate.

c. Questions that help clarify and deepen the subject:

(1) What is temptation?

(2) What is sin?

Prepare these questions in view of the emphasis the group needs most. Have Bible verses ready to help find the right answers. Ask these questions at the proper place in the discussion under the questions mentioned above in 5a (in this instance in 5a3 and 5a4).

d. Questions which stimulate application:

(1) What do you consider the most important warning in this story?

(2) How does this affect your life personally?

Since questions on application can be asked last in the Bible discussion, you can, going around the circle, expect each member of the group to give his personal answer. Words to keep in mind while asking questions are: what, how, why, when.

6. Make a time schedule for yourself to guarantee that every part of the discussion receives sufficient attention. Reserve enough time for those points you think of utmost importance. Since the last question of the Bible study is an application question, you may want to emphasize it.

7. Shy participants often can be drawn into the discussion by asking them to read a Bible verse. It is difficult to control those who want to dominate the discussion. Calling for contributions from others often helps. "What do others think?" Sometimes it is necessary to talk privately with the over-talkative person, explaining the necessity of group participation. Getting back on track when the subject begins to wander can be done by saying, "Perhaps we could discuss this further after the study," or "Let us, as we agreed, try to stick to our subject of the study."

8. Sharing the application is the most important part of your discussion. Be sure to allow sufficient time for each person present to answer the last stated question. The answer to that question should be personal, specific and practical. Example of an application in connection with Eve could be, "The most important warning to me is that I must be sure that I can have victory over temptation. I have decided, therefore, to read the Bible daily. I will begin today by reading . . . ."

9. If you close the discussion with a time of prayer, pray about the things you have discussed. For example, pray for your own application or for someone else's. Don't force anything. Encourage short prayers. Someone who is too shy to pray aloud could enter in by saying, "Amen." As the openness of the group increases, so will the prayer. Then other points can be added for intercession.

10. Close with the promise that at the beginning of the next meeting time will be given for sharing experiences in connection with your group's applications.

These guidelines can be used for all the group discussions about the women in this book.

Biography

Gien Karssen was raised in a Christian home and became a Christian at the age of 12 as a result of her parents' lives and training. After she had been married only six weeks, the Germans interned her husband in a concentration camp where he died. Just before his death he had inscribed Luke 9:62 in his diary, "But Jesus said to him, 'No one, after putting his hand to the plow and looking back, is fit for the kingdom of God.'" This verse challenged Gien and has given purpose and direction to her life. Using this Scripture as a basis, she found it easier to face difficulties, cancel her own desires and want God's will only.

She met Dawson Trotman, founder of The Navigators, in 1948 in Doorn, Holland. She started the Navigator ministry there by translating the Navigators *Topical Memory System* into Dutch and handling all the enrollments. Over the years she has worked in many capacities with The Navigators. Women who have been personally helped by Gien Karssen can be found on almost every continent of the globe.

Gien is a popular speaker, Bible study leader and trainer, and has many years of experience as free-lance writer for Christian periodicals in Europe. *Her Name Is Woman* is her first book. She has also written *Her Name Is Woman* Book 2, *Beside Still Waters* and *The Man Who Was Different.*

1

*"The woman was made of a rib out of the side
of Adam; not made out of his head to rule over him,
nor out of his feet to be trampled upon by him,
but out of his side to be equal with him,
under his arm to be protected, and near his
heart to be beloved."* Matthew Henry*

Eve,
the mother of all living

Genesis 1:27,28 And God created man in His own image, in the image of God He created him; male and female He created them. And God blessed them; and God said to them, "Be fruitful and multiply, and fill the earth, and subdue it; and rule over the fish of the sea and over the birds of the sky, and over every living thing that moves on the earth."

Genesis 2:18 Then the Lord God said, "It is not good for the man to be alone; I will make him a helper suitable for him."

Genesis 2:20-25 And the man gave names to all the cattle, and to the birds of the sky, and to every beast of the field, but for Adam there was not found a helper suitable for him. So the Lord God caused a deep sleep to fall upon the man, and he slept; then He took one of his ribs, and closed up the flesh at that place. And the Lord God fashioned into a woman the rib which He had taken from the man, and brought her to the man. And the man said, "This is now bone of my bones, and flesh of my flesh; she shall be called Woman because she was taken out of Man." For this cause a man shall leave his father and his mother, and shall cleave to his wife; and they shall become one flesh. And the man and his wife were both naked and were not ashamed.

*Henry,Matthew. *A Commentary on the Whole Bible,* Vol. 1,
Fleming H. Revell, Old Tappan, N.J.

Genesis 3:1-20 Now the serpent was more crafty than any beast of the field which the Lord God had made. And he said to the woman, "Indeed, has God said, 'You shall not eat from any tree of the garden'?" And the woman said to the serpent, "From the fruit of the trees of the garden we may eat; but from the fruit of the tree which is in the middle of the gardenn God has said, 'You shall not eat from it or touch it or touch it, lest you die.' "

And the serpent said to the woman, "You surely shall not die! "For God knows that in the day you eat from it your eyes will be opened, and you will be like God, knowing good and evil." When the woman saw that the tree was good for food, and that it was a delight to the eyes, and that the tree was desirable to make one wise, she took from its fruit and ate; and she gave also to her husband with her, and he ate. Then the eyes of both of them were opened, and they knew that they were naked; and they sewed fig leaves together and made themselves loin coverings.

And they heard the sound of the Lord God walking in the garden in the cool of the day, and the man and his wife hid themselves from the presence of the Lord God among the trees of the garden. Then the Lord God called to the man, and said to him, "Where are you?" And he said, "I heard the sound of Thee in the garden, and I was afraid because I was naked; so I hid myself." And He said, "Who told you that you were naked? Have you eaten from the tree of which I commanded you not to eat?" And the man said, "The woman whom Thou gavest to be with me, she gave me from the tree, and I ate." Then the Lord God said to the woman, "What is this you have done?" And the woman said, "The serpent deceived me, and I ate." And the Lord God said to the serpent, "Because you have done this, cursed are you more than all cattle, and more than every beast of the field; on your belly shall you go, and dust shall you eat all the days of your life; and I will put enmity between you and the woman, and between your seed and her seed; He shall bruise you on the head, and you shall bruise Him on the heel." To the woman He said, "I will greatly multiply your pain in childbirth, in pain you shall bring forth children; yet your desire shall be for your husband, and he shall rule over you." Then to Adam He said, "Because you have listened to the voice of your wife, and have eaten from the tree about which I commanded you, saying, 'You shall not eat from it'; cursed is the ground because of you; in toil you shall eat of it all the days of your life. Both thorns and thistles it shall grow for you; and you shall eat the plants of the field; by the sweat of your face you shall eat bread, till you return to the ground, because from it you were taken; for you are dust, and to dust you shall return." Now the man called his wife's name Eve, because she was the mother of all the living.

She was captivated by all she saw—everything around her was perfect. The nature she saw was new and refreshing. The air she breathed was pure and unspoiled. The water she drank was clear and sparkling. Every animal lived harmoniously with all others.

Her marriage was perfect—her fellowship with God and her husband were a daily joy. Eve had everything anyone could desire.

Then one day a voice in the garden asked her, "Did God tell you that you should not eat the fruit of any tree in the garden?"

Why, she wondered, *haven't I ever noticed the special beauty of the tree which stands in the middle of the garden? And why does my entire happiness suddenly seem to depend on eating its fruit? Eating something so desirable can only be good—*

Her desire was aroused. She didn't notice that she was being deceived—that God's Word had been twisted—that God's love was being doubted.

Eve didn't know that the one speaking to her was Satan in disguise.[1] He was and had been a liar and a murderer from the beginning,[2] desiring to deceive people.[3] He didn't quote God precisely, but used his own words.[4]

His attack on God's Word should have warned her not to listen to him. She could still have escaped at this phase of her temptation.[5] For although she was on dangerous ground, she had been created with a will which was capable of withstanding the tempter. She didn't have to give Satan the opportunity to deceive her by listening to him.[6] She had a choice. But, unfortunately, she listened to him. Even worse, she answered him. This marked the beginning of her fall.

Like Satan, Eve also twisted the words of God. She added, "Neither shall you touch it . . ." to what God said, although God had not said anything about touching. Then she weakened His stress on death by omitting the word "shall."

Satan's first blow was successful. Eve was willing to listen to him, to linger with him. This increased his boldness. He blatantly

---

1. Revelation 20:2; II Corinthians 11:14   4. Genesis 2:16,17
2. John 8:44   5. James 4:7
3. I Peter 5:8   6. Ephesians 4:27

called God a liar. He portrayed God as Someone who wanted to subdue man and to curtail his happiness, since He had the power to do so.

"Die?" he railed. "You won't die at all. You will be happier than you ever dreamed. You will be like God." He continued to tempt her, drawing her toward independence. His call to disobedience was fatal to Eve. Her resistance had been broken when she took time to argue with Satan. She stretched forward and took the fruit which her heart desired.

By then, the evil could not be stopped. She had become so entangled in the nets of the deceiver that she could not escape. She ate the fruit. But that was not the end of the matter. The woman who was deceived in turn became a deceiver. Eve entangled her husband in her sin. Without protest he accepted the fruit from her and ate it.

At that moment her entire life changed.

The creation God had made was ideal. It was so perfect that He was satisfied with it Himself [7] and stressed this fact after every deed of creation.

Yet something was missing. "It is not good for a man to be alone. I will make him a helpmeet," said the Lord God. After both man and woman were created, God's work was complete and "very good."[8]

Eve was a creature carved by the hand of God. She was created equal to her husband. Their only difference was sex. She was unique.

As a human being, she, like Adam, was gifted with reason and understanding. Therefore, she was his partner in conversation. And like him she had a personal relationship with and was expected to be obedient to her Creator. Along with Adam, God made Eve accountable for executing the same tasks. In her own specific way, she was to help fill and subdue the earth. She had a unique relationship with her husband. She shared her life with him. She completed him. Her physical structure made her fit him, so that together they could execute God's command to multiply.

Although completed after Adam, Eve was certainly not an

7. Genesis 1:10,12,18,21,25
8. Genesis 1:31

"afterthought." She was as much a part of God's original plan as Adam was. She couldn't function without him and he could not do without her.[9] Within their marriage, Eve was subject to Adam.[10] Adam had been appointed by God to exercise leadership in order to guarantee social order, for God is a God of order.

In the Trinity, the Son is in no way inferior to the Father (John 5:18; Philippians 2:6), yet He is subject to Him. In marriage, a husband and wife are of equal importance (Galatians 3:28), but the wife's role is to be subject to her husband as Christ is to God (I Corinthians 11:3). Thus, in God's order it is fitting for a wife to subordinate herself voluntarily to her husband.

As husband and wife, Adam and Eve formed a new nucleus: a couple. This couple was characterized by its own personality. It was not the sum of two individuals; it was its own new entity. It is God's plan that the marriage partners should live together in complete harmony—that they feel at ease with one another, one in a bond maintained by mutual love and respect.[11]

Eve realized how bitterly she had been deceived. She first noticed this in her relationship to Adam. They had always been at ease with one another as God had created them to be. But now they were suddenly shy and defenseless. The protection of their innocence was gone. They discovered they could not have a free and easy relationship. They began to hide things from one another. They discovered that they not only stood naked to one another— they were naked before God! Their purity was gone. Their sinless nature had been destroyed. Their intimate relationship with God was broken. Instead of becoming like Him as Satan had promised, they became afraid of Him and fled from Him.

Then God entered this devastating situation. He took the initiative to look for them. How lovingly He greeted them. He started with a question, not an accusation. He gave them a chance to acknowledge their sin, but they failed to see their opportunity. He called Adam responsible,[12] since he was the head of the family. Though he was present, Adam did not stop Eve from committing the sin. In fact, he joined her. And he blamed her. "The woman You gave me did it." Adam almost sounded as if he blamed God for giving Eve to him.

Eve passed the guilt on to someone else, too. She blamed the serpent, although if she had been honest with herself, she would have had to admit that she had voluntarily accepted his offer. It

9. I Corinthians 11:11,12   11. Ephesians 5:21
10. Ephesians 5:22-24   12. Romans 5:12,14

was true, he had misled her, but she had sinned of her own free will. She had failed the test offered to her as a human being to obey God voluntarily out of love.

The judgment of God that followed revealed to her the catastrophic impact of her deed. Not only the beautiful garden of Eden, but the entire world was cursed. The soil, once without weeds, would now produce thorns and thistles. The animals were cursed. The tranquility of the animal kingdom over which Adam and Eve had ruled together was marred. The wolf and lamb would no longer eat peacefully together. The stronger would rule the weaker. The beautiful paradise in which they could have lived happily forever had, with one quick blow, become a lost paradise. They were ordered to leave quickly, so they wouldn't eat from the tree of life and thus be forced to live forever as sinful people.[13]

Eve, who had completed God's creation—who was the last link in the chain of happiness on earth—had thrown this happiness away by her disobedience.

Her joy of motherhood would be tempered by pain and trouble. The sting of lordship would now affect her relationship with her husband. He would now rule over her because of sin.

And though Adam and Eve did not die instantly after their sin in the garden, the institution of death was a result. In a second they had become mortal human beings, subject to death.

But far worse than natural death was spiritual death, the vacuum of separation from God.[14] This, most of all, Eve painfully experienced in her innermost self.

Eve was lonely and had a difficult time during childbirth. Being the first woman on earth she had no mother, no sister, no friend who could share her feelings. There was no one to go to for advice, no other woman who could help her with the delivery. And what a strange experience, to become a mother when you have never been a child yourself. What do you do with a child? In these trying circumstances it is no wonder that Eve fell back on God. "I have given birth to a man with the help of the Lord,"[15] she said, and smiled at her baby, Cain.

She and Adam were not the only ones to be punished for sinning against God. Satan's punishment was far greater. He was told of

13. Genesis 3:22,23
14. Genesis 2:17; Ephesians 2:1
15. Genesis 4:1

his destruction, by Someone named Immanuel, who would be born of Eve's offspring.[16] Was she hoping, was she expecting, that the child in her arms was the promised Messiah?

Eve was a living demonstration of faith—faith that one could never sink so deeply so as not to be able to turn back to God. And hope—hope that God would give new possibilities, no matter how great the sin.

Eve was crushed when Cain killed her second son. She realized that she had brought a sinful man into the world. He was a murderer. The terrible extent of her deed in the garden became even more starkly clear to her. She had passed on death—spiritually and physically—to Adam, and he to every person born.[17] No human would ever again live in innocence, as she once had. Each person born would sin not only by choice, but also because of an inner urging. Everyone would face an unending battle between good and evil. Everyone would be separated by sin from God. There would be no exceptions.

Again and again Satan appeals to the desires of man, trying to entice him. Sin and death will enter the scene each time one gives in to his own desires.[18] In every generation there will be people like Eve who are moved by the desire to have what the eyes see and to satisfy the desires of pride.[19] Satan tries to move every person against God just as he did Eve. He stirs up rebellion and ingratitude in order to cause men to fall like he fell—from pride.[20]

Even many, many years after Eden when man is redeemed by Jesus Christ[21] and everyone who personally believes in Him again has access to God,[22] the best of men will realize that while they want to do good, they are drawn toward evil.[23] Only Jesus Christ—the Announced One—has proven that a man can conquer temptation if he clings to and lives by the Word of God.[24]

As a result of Adam and Eve's sin, the tears, mourning and pain men experience now will continue until a new kingdom.[25] And until that time, every human will be plagued with sin. Until then, every person will be urgently warned not to follow Eve's example.[26] For Eve, the mother of all living, provides a frightening example. She is the woman who admitted sin into the world when she allowed Satan to make her doubt God's Word and His love.

16. Isaiah 7:14
17. Romans 3:10-12,23; 6:23a
18. James 1:14,15
19. I John 2:16

20. Isaiah 14:12-15
21. I John 2:2
22. John 1:12,13
23. Romans 7:15-19

24. Matthew 4:1-11
25. Revelation 21:1,4
26. II Corinthians 11:3

Eve, the mother of all living
(Genesis 1:27,28; 2:18,20-25; 3:1-20)

Questions:

1. Read Genesis 1 and 2. How and why was Eve created?
2. Who was the serpent? (Revelation 20:2; John 8:44) What tactics did he apply when he deceived Eve?
3. In what ways do you consider him to be still at work according to Matthew 4:1-11 and I John 2:16?
4. Can a human being withstand temptation? If so, how?
5. Describe the situation in which Eve lived before the fall.
6. How was that situation afterward? Mention all the changes you can find.
7. What do you consider to be the most far-reaching result of Eve's sin?
8. What do you think is the most important warning in this story? How does this affect your life personally?

2

*"Faith is confidence, reliance, trust. It is the
sixth sense which enables us to apprehend
the invisible but real spiritual realm. Within
this realm its dealings are directly with God."*
J. Oswald Sanders*

Sarah,
the princess whose name is recorded with honor

Genesis 18:1-15 Now the Lord appeared to him by the oaks of
Mamre, while he was sitting at the tent door in the heat of the day.
And when he lifted up his eyes and looked, behold, three men were
standing opposite him; and when he saw them, he ran from the tent
door to meet them, and bowed himself to the earth, and said, "My
lord, if now I have found favor in your sight, please do not pass your
servant by. Please let a little water be brought and wash your feet,
and rest yourselves under the tree; and I will bring a piece of bread,
that you may refresh yourselves; after that you may go on, since
you have visited your servant." And they said, "So do, as you have
said." So Abraham hurried into the tent to Sarah, and said,
"Quickly, prepare three measures of fine flour, knead it, and make
bread cakes." Abraham also ran to the herd, and took a tender and
choice calf, and gave it to the servant; and he hurried to prepare it.
And he took curds and milk and the calf which he had prepared,
and placed it before them; and he was standing by them under the
tree as they ate.

Then they said to him, "Where is Sarah your wife?" And he said,
"Behold, in the tent." And he said, "I will surely return to you at this
time next year; and behold, Sarah your wife shall have a son." And
Sarah was listening at the tent door, which was behind him. Now

*Sanders, J. Oswald. *Mighty Faith,*
© 1971, Moody Press, Chicago, Illinois.

Abraham and Sarah were old, advanced in age; Sarah was past childbearing. And Sarah laughed to herself, saying, "After I have become old, shall I have pleasure, my lord being old also?" And the Lord said to Abraham, "Why did Sarah laugh, saying, 'Shall I indeed bear a child, when I am so old?' Is anything too difficult for the Lord? At the appointed time I will return to you, at this time next year, and Sarah shall have a son." Sarah denied it however, saying, "I did not laugh"; for she was afraid. And He said, "No, but you did laugh."

Genesis 21:1-13 Then the Lord took note of Sarah as He had said, and the Lord did for Sarah as He had promised. So Sarah conceived and bore a son to Abraham in his old age, at the appointed time of which God had spoken to him. And Abraham called the name of his son who was born to him, whom Sarah bore to him, Isaac. Then Abraham circumcised his son Isaac when he was eight days old, as God had commanded him. Now Abraham was one hundred years old when his son Isaac was born to him. And Sarah said, "God has made laughter for me; everyone who hears will laugh with me." And she said, "Who would have said to Abraham that Sarah would nurse children? Yet I have borne him a son in his old age."

And the child grew and was weaned, and Abraham made a great feast on the day that Isaac was weaned. Now Sarah saw the son of Hagar the Egyptian, whom she had borne to Abraham, mocking. Therefore she said to Abraham, "Drive out this maid and her son, for the son of this maid shall not be an heir with my son Isaac." And the matter distressed Abraham greatly because of his son. But God said to Abraham, "Do not be distressed because of the lad and your maid; whatever Sarah tells you, listen to her, for through Isaac your descendants shall be named. And of the son of the maid I will make a nation also, because he is your descendant."

Hebrews 11:11 By faith even Sarah herself received ability to conceive, even beyond the proper time of life, since she considered Him faithful who had promised.

I Peter 3:6 Thus Sarah obeyed Abraham, calling him lord, and you have become her children if you do what is right without being frightened by any fear.

The scene is Hebron, two thousand years before Christ.

Sarah laughs, but not because she is happy. She laughs, because of what she has heard—that she, a woman of 89, would give birth to a child! A son. Impossible!

She and her husband are too old for a baby. It is biologically impossible that she could bring forth a child although they had been waiting for many years. They had been convinced that God Himself had promised them a son 25 years ago, but the promise had not been fulfilled. They must have been mistaken. Sarah reflected back on those years. . . .

They had lived in Ur, a center of culture and commerce in South Mesopotamia. Though Ur had passed its peak in history, it had still provided a flourishing existence. Its craftsmen were surpassed only by those of Egypt. The ships in the harbor brought goods from the East in exchange for locally grown grains. Many citizens were rich and lived in spacious homes.

She and Abraham had enjoyed their time there, living among relatives and friends. But one day their lives were radically changed. God had appeared to Abraham.[1] His appearance had been so glorious[2] that it had removed all doubt as to who He was. This was the true God, not the moon god Sin, whom Abraham's forefathers had worshipped.[3]

God had ordered Abraham to leave his land and relatives to go to a country which He would point out. The order had been linked with a promise, "And I will make you a great nation, and I will bless you, and make your name great; and so you shall be a blessing; and I will bless those who bless you, and the one who curses you I will curse, and in you all the families of the earth shall be blessed."[4]

Abraham had obeyed immediately. And Sarah had adjusted to the decision. They had suddenly become seminomads, instead of citizens of a wealthy, comfortable city.

As with most women, she hadn't found it easy to leave her home and loved ones behind to face an unknown future. But she had obeyed her husband and trusted the God who had spoken to him.

For months they had traveled, moving slowly across the land

1. Genesis 11:31-12:5   3. Joshua 24:2
2. Acts 7:2,3   4. Genesis 12:2,3

because of their animals. Finally, they had arrived in Haran, 600 miles northwest. They had stayed there a long time, and life again became a little more comfortable, though not as luxurious as it had been in Ur. However, it had been considerably better than their previous roving existence.

But then there had been another move. This time to the southwest. A little more of her security had crumbled away. Terah, their father, had died. She was Abraham's half sister. But that wasn't unusual since opportunities to marry in those days were so limited, one often had to look for a partner within the innermost family circle. With their father's death and the absence of those relatives who stayed behind in Haran,[5] life had become even more lonely. Only Lot, a cousin, had traveled with them.

Despite their losses, two things had remained unchanged. First, they had continued to believe the promises of God. They felt they would still have the child, even though they were getting older, Abraham being 75 and she, 65. Second, they had continued to experience a lasting respect and love toward one another.

It hadn't all been easy. Like Abraham, she had a strong personality with a well-developed character. She had done her best to adjust herself to her husband and to obey him. She definitely had a mind of her own, yet she had been able to give herself to him because of an inner freedom.

Yes, as she reflected on it, her relationship with her husband was determined by her relationship with God. Her trust in God had made her a faithful, strong woman, enabling her to stand in life undaunted and steadfast, living in harmony with her husband.[6]

The father of all believers and his wife unknowingly showed through their marriage a foreshadowing of Christ's relationship with His future Church (Ephesians 5:22-33).

Because she had obeyed him and given him first place, he, in turn, respected her, listened to her advice and honored her with his friendship. They were friends as well as lovers, discussing matters of mutual, daily concern. Since they were open to God and to one another, their marriage and spiritual lives were strong.

Time had passed, but they still had no child. Meanwhile, they had arrived at Shechem where God appeared to Abraham again

5. Genesis 24:4,10; 27:43
6. I Peter 3:1-7

and said, "To your descendants I will give this land."[7]

At last they had reached their destination. And they had still hoped for the promised child. In gratitude Abraham had built an altar to God. But because a severe famine came upon the land, Abraham had moved southward in order to get food for his family and animals. He had done this on his own, without asking God's counsel. They had gone to Egypt. Had they gone in a direction not pleasing to God?[8]

It had not been easy in Egypt. Because Sarah was beautiful, Abraham had feared for his life, feeling that the Egyptians would kill him in order to get her. So Abraham had said to her, "Please tell them you are my sister so that they won't try to kill me."[9] He had taken refuge in a lie, because of fear. Yet he was a man who had trusted God implicitly for years. *What about his love for me?* she had wondered.

It was true that in the beginning of their wanderings they had agreed to use this tactic. They had quieted their consciences with the fact that actually it wasn't a lie.[10] Theoretically this had sounded acceptable, but in practice she had felt betrayed.

Just as Abraham had expected, her beauty had been noticed. She ended up in the pharaoh's harem. Abraham's fear of dying had not only endangered her purity, but she had felt he acted in disregard to the promise of their child.

But the God in whom she had trusted intervened. Through torment and great plagues, God had made the situation clear to the heathen king.[11] She had lost some confidence in her husband as a result of the whole affair. Momentarily, he had left his pedestal. A bit more of her security had crumbled away.

They had then returned to the land God had promised them, bringing with them a young Egyptian slave girl, Hagar. As the years passed without the promised child, Abraham had wondered if perhaps an adopted son would be God's solution. Perhaps the son should be Eliezer, the most important man in his household.[12]

But that was not God's plan. God had promised that a son conceived by Sarah would be the heir. The promise of a descendant remained unchanged and was confirmed by an oath.[13] Though God had repeated His promises, He had been slow in fulfilling them.

7. Genesis 12:6,7
8. Exodus 33:14,15
9. Genesis 12:13
10. Genesis 20:12,13
11. Genesis 12:10-20
12. Genesis 15:1-4
13. Genesis 15:5-21

She knew from experience that to live a life of faith she was not only asked to abstain from human security, but also to be patient. Faith and patience went together. They couldn't be purchased easily like merchandise but had to be learned through the difficult school of life. They needed exercise[14] and were proven by actual deeds. She and Abraham had had to learn that faith is to be anchored in the solid ground of God's promises and not in the quicksand of human possibilities.

But she had become impatient. Taking into account that her childbearing years were past, she had suggested Abraham take Hagar, the Egyptian maid, as a concubine.[15] Outwardly, she had adapted herself to the customs of the time. After all, such things occurred frequently. Probably she could have legally defended her action by referring to her wedding contract in which she had promised her husband a son. But what she had done was wrong because it lacked faith.

Her self-denial had led her to great sacrifice. She could have offered the excuse that God had not said that the promised son would be her own child. But had she made an unnecessary sacrifice because she wanted desperately to see God's promise fulfilled at any cost and at her chosen time? The long time of waiting, ten years by then, had been nearly unbearable. Her real problem probably hadn't been that her patience wore thin, but that she had sought the solution herself. She had taken her lot into her own hands and had paid heavily for it.

What had moved Abraham to listen to her? That still was not clear. But like Adam before him, he had plucked the bitter fruit of listening to the wrong suggestion of his wife.[16] Oh, why had he listened?

The consequences were evident almost immediately. The sin of unbelief and impatience had begun bearing fruit even before the child was long in Hagar's womb. The patriarchal home had been torn by discontent and lack of peace. Hagar had developed a feeling of superiority.

She, Sarah, had forgotten that she had taken the initiative in the unhappy plan. Because she had departed from God, she had neglected to search her own heart or to repent. Instead, she had blamed her husband. She had humiliated Hagar so deeply that if

14. Hebrews 6:13-15
15. Genesis 16
16. Genesis 3:17

God had not interceded the young woman probably would have died. Sarah had degraded herself. She had learned what destructive powers a person can unleash in himself when he wanders away from God.

She had wanted to win time. There was no one to know whether or not this resulted in actually losing time instead. She did know, however, that it had been 13 years before God had revealed Himself to Abraham. How had he felt during that time?

Abraham was still very busy waiting on his guests, who had suddenly come from nowhere and stood before him. During their visit Sarah helped by preparing the meal. When time had come to serve, she had remained in the background as was the custom in the East where the world was dominated by men.

Her attention had been aroused when she heard one of them ask, "Where is your wife, Sarah?" This had caused her to start musing as she had walked toward the entrance of the tent. *Who are these men? How do they know my name? What further do they know about me?* she wondered.

Abraham had told them, "She is in the tent." Then had come the surprising statement, "I will return to you in a year; and behold Sarah, your wife, shall have a son."

The men were still sitting with their backs toward the tent, and Sarah felt she wouldn't be noticed. She was alone with her thoughts. In her heart she laughed about these words. They were very polite, actually. They were gentlemen. They showed their gratitude for the hospitality by courteously promising the host a son.

Suddenly her musing was over as she was brought abruptly back to reality. Startled, she heard her unspoken thoughts said in words. The man asked, "Why did Sarah laugh, asking, 'How shall I bear a son at my age?'" He followed immediately with the impressive words, "Is there anything too difficult for the Lord?"

The Lord? The Lord?

Then she recognized Him, as Abraham had already recognized Him. Hadn't her husband addressed the three people in the singular with, "My Lord?"

The Lord Himself had descended from heaven to talk to her, to confirm the promise to her personally, "At this time next year I will return and Sarah shall have a son."

Totally shocked, she denied her lack of faith and said, "I did not laugh." She knew His reply before He made it, "Yes, you did."

Why hadn't the Lord addressed me directly? she mused. Because it is an Eastern way of life to speak to a woman through her husband? Or did He want to remind Abraham that he, like his wife, had laughed in unbelief? Not too long ago God had repeated the promise of a son to him.[17] For Abraham also had lost hope of ever receiving a son from Sarah. He was satisfied with Ishmael, and had begged that he would be acceptable to God.

For the first time God said explicitly that the son of the promise would be the son of Sarah. As proof of this He had changed their names. Instead of Abram, "father of height," from now on his name would be Abraham, the "father of a multitude." Sarai was changed to Sarah, meaning "princess." The Lord had not considered it sufficient to tell only Abraham that his time of waiting was coming to an end. He had also come to tell Sarah personally.

The next year, at the time appointed by God, a son was born. The name that God gave him, Isaac, means "laughing one." As long as they lived, Isaac would remind his parents of the fact that in unbelief they had put a question mark behind his name, which God had changed into an exclamation mark.

The year that preceded Isaac's birth was not a spotless one for Abraham and Sarah, even though God had taken Abraham into His confidence like a friend (Isaiah 41:8; Genesis 18:16-19). The lie of Egypt had repeated itself. See Genesis 20.

The results of Sarah's mistake of allowing Hagar to become Abraham's concubine continued to be very serious. Because Ishmael had mocked Isaac at his weaning feast, Sarah urged Abraham to send Hagar and Ishmael away. There was sorrow in Abraham's heart, for he also suffered from his participation in the sin. God told him, however, to listen to Sarah. So he sent the Egyptian away with his child. God loved them too as history has proven, but there developed a distinct separation between the descendants of Isaac and Ishmael. Sarah only lived 37

17. Genesis 17

more years after Isaac's birth, so she did not see the misery and sorrow that was released by the descendants of Abraham's two sons.

The Arabs, the descendants of Ishmael, and the Jews, the descendants of Isaac, have become lasting enemies. After many centuries the problems in the Middle East are still awaiting a solution.

How very sad for Sarah that her one deed of impatience had such far-reaching effects and that her memory had to be marred by this. But the Bible doesn't finish her story in a minor key.

The first woman presented in the portrait gallery of the heroes of faith in Hebrews 11 is Sarah. She is recorded with honor because of the faith she did have, not because of her failures.

Her faith, majestically illustrated at the birth of Isaac, grew during her long life. Life had requested many sacrifices from Sarah. She abstained from many things she loved and wanted. She experienced hardships and disappointments—all without murmuring. She was flexible in changing situations. She adjusted herself to her husband. By her obedience to Abraham, she allowed him to obey God.

Scientists have discovered that bad emotions can make a person ill. They also say that healthy emotions governed by a sense of happiness, contentment and an unshaken belief in God can cause physical beauty, good health and a long life.

Could that have been the secret of Sarah's outward beauty and vitality? Peter praises Sarah for her inner beauty and challenges all woman to follow her example. For Sarah truly is a princess among women.

Sarah, the princess whose name is recorded with honor
(Genesis 18:1-15; 21:1-13; Hebrews 11:11; I Peter 3:6)

Questions:
1. Read Hebrews 11:11 again. Why is Sarah's name mentioned among the heroes of faith?

2. Compare I Peter 3:6 with Ephesians 5:22-33. What strikes you about her relationship with her husband?
3. Which experiences in Sarah's life, do you think gave her faith a chance to grow? (Study also the references quoted from Genesis 11, 12 and 20.)
4. What do you consider the greatest challenge of her faith?
5. What proof is there that Sarah's faith also experienced low points? What negative characteristics do you see then? (Also read Genesis 16.)
6. What results do you see stemming from Sarah's impatience?
7. Ishmael was the forefather of the Arabs. What results of Sarah's life do you see continuing today?
8. What lessons have you learned from Sarah? Choose the most important one from them and decide how you can apply it to your life.

3

*"A rare find is an able wife—she
is worth far more than rubies!"*
Solomon*

Rebekah,
a woman with great potential, yet . . .

Genesis 24:1-28 Now Abraham was old, advanced in age; and the
Lord had blessed Abraham in every way. And Abraham said to his
servant, the oldest of his household, who had charge of all that he
owned, "Please place your hand under my thigh, and I will make
you swear by the Lord, the God of heaven and the God of earth, that
you shall not take a wife for my son from the daughters of the
Canaanites, among whom I live, but you shall go to my country and
to my relatives, and take a wife for my son Isaac." And the servant
said to him, "Suppose the woman will not be willing to follow me to
this land; should I take your son back to the land from where you
came?" Then Abraham said to him, "Beware lest you take my son
back there! The Lord, the God of heaven, who took me from my
father's house and from the land of my birth, and who spoke to me,
and who swore to me, saying, 'To your descendants I will give this
land,' He will send His angel before you, and you will take a wife for
my son from there. But if the woman is not willing to follow you,
then you will be free from this my oath; only do not take my son
back there." So the servant placed his hand under the thigh of
Abraham his master, and swore to him concerning this matter.

Then the servant took ten camels from the camels of his master,
and set out with a variety of good things of his master's in his hand;

*Proverbs 31:10. Moffatt, James. *The Bible, A New Translation,*
© 1935, Harper & Row, Publishers, New York, N.Y.

and he arose, and went to Mesopotamia, to the city of Nahor. And he made the camels kneel down outside the city by the well of water at evening time, the time when women go out to draw water. And he said, "O Lord, the God of my master Abraham, please grant me success today, and show lovingkindness to my master Abraham. Behold, I am standing by the spring, and the daughters of the men of the city are coming out to draw water; now may it be that the girl to whom I say, 'Please let down your jar so that I may drink,' and who answers, 'Drink, and I will water your camels also';—may she be the one whom Thou hast appointed for Thy servant Isaac; and by this I shall know that Thou hast shown lovingkindness to my master." And it came about before he had finished speaking, that behold, Rebekah who was born to Bethuel the son of Milcah, the wife of Abraham's brother Nahor, came out with her jar on her shoulder. And the girl was very beautiful, a virgin, and no man had had relations with her; and she went down to the spring and filled her jar, and came up. Then the servant ran to meet her, and said, "Please let me drink a little water from your jar." And she said, "Drink, my lord"; and she quickly lowered her jar to her hand, and gave him a drink. Now when she had finished giving him a drink, she said, "I will draw also for your camels until they have finished drinking." So she quickly emptied her jar into the trough, and ran back to the well to draw, and she drew for all his camels. Meanwhile, the man was gazing at her in silence, to know whether the Lord had made his journey successful or not. Then it came about, when the camels had finished drinking, that the man took a gold ring weighing a half-shekel and two bracelets for her wrists weighing ten shekels in gold, and said, "Whose daughter are you? Please tell me, is there room for us to lodge in your father's house?" And she said to him, "I am the daughter of Bethuel, the son of Milcah, whom she bore to Nahor." Again she said to him, "We have plenty of both straw and feed, and room to lodge in." Then the man bowed low and worshipped the Lord. And he said, "Blessed be the Lord, the God of my master Abraham, who has not forsaken His lovingkindness and His truth toward my master; as for me, the Lord has guided me in the way to the house of my master's brothers."

Then the girl ran and told her mother's household about these things.

Genesis 24:58-67 Then they called Rebekah and said to her, "Will you go with this man?" And she said, "I will go." Thus they sent away their sister Rebekah and her nurse with Abraham's servant and his men. And they blessed Rebekah and said to her, "May you, our sister, become thousands of ten thousands, and may your descendants possess the gate of those who hate them."

Then Rebekah arose with her maids, and they mounted the camels and followed the man. So the servant took Rebekah and departed. Now Isaac had come from going to Beer-lahai-roi; for he was living in the Negev. And Isaac went out to meditate in the field toward evening; and he lifted up his eyes and looked, and behold, camels were coming. And Rebekah lifted up her eyes, and when she saw Isaac she dismounted from the camel. And she said to the servant, "Who is that man walking in the field to meet us?" And the servant said, "He is my master." Then she took her veil and covered herself. And the servant told Isaac all the things that he had done. Then Isaac brought her into his mother Sarah's tent, and he took Rebekah, and she became his wife; and he loved her; thus Isaac was comforted after his mother's death.

I. The marriage proposal

It began much like a fairy tale. A much desired bachelor, the only son of a wealthy father and the heir to a massive fortune,[1] was looking for a wife. Even before his birth God had promised that he would have numerous offspring. God had also said that He would make an everlasting covenant with him and his descendants.[2] Therefore, the mother of these children and grandmother of the children's children needed to be chosen very carefully.

Isaac was the young bachelor. His father, Abraham, made all the preparations for the wedding—he even chose the bride. He had sent a man whom he could trust with this delicate commission— probably Eliezer, the steward of his house[3]—to Haran in Mesopotamia, where Abraham had lived earlier. Some of his relatives were still there. It seemed to him that someone from within the family circle would be the best guarantee for a harmonious marriage bond. They would have the same background and mutual understanding.

Though living in Canaan, Isaac was not allowed to marry a local woman, because the Canaanites were under the curse of God.[4] They were heathen, for they did not worship the God of Isaac, and

1. Genesis 24:34-36   3. Genesis 15:2-4
2. Genesis 17:19; 12:2,3   4. Genesis 9:22-27

marrying an unbeliever would create an unequal pair in God's sight.[5]

Abraham, who desired a wife of God's choice for his son, was convinced that marriages should be made in heaven. He believed that God was personally interested in the joining together of two people. After all, hadn't He created a special wife for Adam, someone with whom the first man could enjoy an optimum of happiness?[6]

He believed that God had also selected a wife for Isaac. As a father he could give his son riches, but only the Lord could give him an understanding wife[7]—a good wife is a gift and blessing from the Lord.[8]

Abraham was certain that God Himself would be in charge of the trip if he asked Him.[9] Thus he encouraged his steward with the promise that the Lord God would send His angel[10] before him to ensure contact with the proper woman.

After a 550-mile journey Eliezer arrived in Haran where Nahor, Abraham's brother, lived. He did two things upon arrival. He prayed for help and then, being practical, he went to the most common gathering place in town, the water well. It was nearing evening. Soon the women would come to fetch water.

How would he select the right wife for Isaac from the many who would come to the well? Which one had God destined to be the wife of the son of his master? Everything depended upon God's leading, so Eliezer proceeded prayerfully.

He prayed for a sign of recognition, "May the girl whom I ask for water and who offers to water my camels also be the wife You desire for Isaac." And knowing that a person can ask God for anything, he asked for success that very day.

In spite of its brevity, this prayer revealed the steward's keen insight. Eastern women were very shy when meeting strange men. Therefore, if a girl responded so frankly to him, he could take this as God's leading.

But was he aware that the answer to his prayer would also reveal certain other qualities about the girl? It was no small thing to draw water for ten camels. Thirty to sixty gallons needed to be drawn and carried. That required good health and physical strength. The woman who was to be next in the chain of many offspring which

5. II Corinthians 6:14
6. Genesis 2:18
7. Proverbs 19:14
8. Proverbs 18:22
9. Proverbs 3:5,6
10. Exodus 23:20

God had promised to Abraham would need to be strong and healthy.

The action would also reveal something about her character. Friendliness and a willingness to serve should be characteristic of Isaac's bride. Efficiency and the ability to do hard work would be beneficial in the nomadic existence she would lead with her husband. It would also be in her favor if she showed initiative when she had ideas of her own.

Isaac, the son of aged parents, had remained a bachelor until after he was 40. He was strongly attached to his mother. He was not a man of great deeds. His wife would need to complement him, having qualities he didn't possess.

Abraham's servant had prayed softly to himself. No one had heard his request but God. He was scarcely finished praying when something inside him warned him to look up. There in front of him he saw a girl with a pitcher on her shoulder. Slender. Youthful. As she approached, he more strongly sensed that she was the answer to his prayer. Here was Isaac's bride!

The day had started like any other for Rebekah. There had been no indication that this would be a history-making day. She had no idea she was about to begin the leading role in a love story that would touch hearts for thousands of years to come. The daily walk to the well was prosaic, like yesterday's and like the day before yesterday's—but this day, when she arrived at the well, she sensed tension in the stranger who watched her approach. It didn't annoy her. She gladly answered his request for water.

Why is my heartbeat so light, so happy—as if it were expecting something? she wondered. It seemed as if something outside her was giving wings to her feet and extra strength to her arms. She wanted to do something especially friendly for this kindly old man. So she volunteered to draw for his camels too. It took a long time before the thirst of all the animals was quenched, yet the light, happy feeling stayed with her. She completed the hard work efficiently.

The searching eyes of the foreigner hadn't left her for an instant. Silently, he scrutinized her.

When the work was completed, he gave her gifts of gold. It surprised her that he would give such a rich gift for the small favor, but she could see, from the people who were with him, that he was a rich man.

"Tell me whose daughter you are."

She noticed the suppressed tension in his voice. When she answered, "I am the daughter of Bethuel. He is the son of Milcah and Nahor," he bowed his head to God and praised Him.

When she heard him mention the well-known name of her great-uncle Abraham in his prayer and realized that this godly man had made his long journey especially to meet her family, she ran home to tell them.

Because of all the excitement, no one slept very well in Bethuel's home that night. They had all come to one conclusion after hearing the man's story—this was the leading of God. They had heard how the search for Isaac's wife was anchored in the promises of the Lord. As Isaac's birth and life were proof of the fulfillment of the promises of God,[11] so was his marriage to be connected with God's promises. His trust in these promises was the reason for Abraham's actions. In sending Eliezer on the search for the bride, Abraham was convinced he was doing God's will and was sure of an answer to his prayers.[12]

Moses later passed on God's commandment that children obey their parents (Deuteronomy 5:16). Solomon suggested getting the advice of others before taking action (Proverbs 20:18). If parents and advisors react positively to a marriage consideration, and if, from its initial stages, the marriage is based on the Word of God and prayer, then as in Rebekah and Isaac's case, one can conclude that God is definitely leading.

Abraham and Eliezer weren't disappointed. God had clearly shown the way.[13] God's leading was further revealed by the agreement of the relatives. In Rebekah's culture marriage was not something to be decided on only by the partners. Others, especially the parents, were involved in counseling.

Though the family had voiced its opinion, the final word was with Rebekah. She gave an unconditional "yes" to the question, "Will you go with this man?" Her answer was a great step in faith. The distance between her future home and her parents' city meant she

11. Romans 4:18-21; Hebrews 11:17-19   13. Psalms 143:8; 32:8
12. I John 5:14,15

probably would never return. It would be a lifetime separation.

Rebekah, the granddaughter of Nahor, exhibited some of the same quality of faith as Nahor's brother Abraham. When she knew God's will, she obeyed unconditionally just as Abraham had. She was prepared to adjust her life to whatever was required of her by her future husband.

They met for the first time in a field. The closeness of the tent had been too much for Isaac. He had gone out to talk with God realizing that the caravan might return any day.

Rebekah saw a man coming toward the caravan. When she learned that he was Isaac, she covered her face with a veil, for a bride in the East never showed her face to the groom until after the wedding ceremony.

Isaac's bride must have reminded him of his mother. Like Sarah, Rebekah was intelligent, energetic, strong-willed and very lovely. She was everything he could desire in a woman. He loved her and she loved him.

Marriage is a symbol of the covenant between God and the Jewish nation (Hosea 2:18,19). In the future it becomes symbolic of Christ and His Church (Ephesians 5:23,24).

History is much more interesting than fairy tales because the people are made of flesh and blood, of emotions and reason, of hope and despair. Rebekah, a young, unknown girl became a participant in the history of Abraham, the father of the Jewish faith, the father of all believers, the friend of God. She entered on the threshold of a future full of promise. What would she make of it?

Rebekah, a woman with great potential, yet . . .
I. The marriage proposal
(Genesis 24:1-28, 58-67)

Questions:
1. Describe briefly how the marriage between Isaac and Rebekah developed.
2. What is marriage a symbol of? (Ephesians 5:23,24,32) What conclusions can you draw from this?

3. Compare Genesis 24:3 with II Corinthians 6:14. What can you conclude from this?
4. What place does prayer have in this story?
5. What strikes you about God's leading? (Also read Psalms 32:8; 143:8.)
6. In what way does the biblical principle set forth in Proverbs 20:18 apply to the development of this marriage?
7. What things can those who are looking for a life partner learn from this story?

"Every wise woman buildeth her house:
but the foolish plucketh it down
with her hands." Solomon*

II. Rebekah takes her lot in her own hands

Genesis 27:1-30 Now it came about, when Isaac was old, and his eyes were too dim to see, that he called his older son Esau and said to him, "My son." And he said to him, "Here I am." And Isaac said, "Behold now, I am old and I do not know the day of my death. Now then, please take your gear, your quiver and your bow, and go out to the field and hunt game for me; and prepare a savory dish for me such as I love, and bring it to me that I may eat, so that my soul may bless you before I die."

And Rebekah was listening while Isaac spoke to his son Esau. So when Esau went to the field to hunt for game to bring home, Rebekah said to her son Jacob, "Behold, I heard your father speak to your brother Esau, saying, 'Bring me some game and prepare a savory dish for me, that I may eat, and bless you in the presence of the Lord before my death.' Now therefore, my son, listen to me as I command you. Go now to the flock and bring me two choice kids from there, that I may prepare them as a savory dish for your father, such as he loves. Then you shall bring it to your father, that he may eat, so that he may bless you before his death." And Jacob answered his mother Rebekah, "Behold, Esau my brother is a hairy man and I am a smooth man. Perhaps my father will feel me, then I shall be as a deceiver in his sight; and I shall bring upon myself a

*Proverbs 14:1 *King James Version*

curse and not a blessing." But his mother said to him, "Your curse be on me, my son; only obey my voice, and go, get them for me." So he went and got them, and brought them to his mother; and his mother made savory food such as his father loved. Then Rebekah took the best garments of Esau her elder son, which were with her in the house, and put them on Jacob her younger son. And she put the skins of the kids on his hands and on the smooth part of his neck. She also gave the savory food and the bread, which she had made, to her son Jacob.

Then he came to his father and said, "My father." And he said, "Here I am. Who are you, my son?" And Jacob said to his father, "I am Esau your first-born; I have done as you told me. Get up, please, sit and eat of my game, that you may bless me." And Isaac said to his son, "How is it that you have it so quickly, my son?" And he said, "Because the Lord your God caused it to happen to me." Then Isaac said to Jacob, "Please come close, that I may feel you, my son, whether you are really my son Esau or not." So Jacob came close to Isaac his father, and he felt him and said, "The voice is the voice of Jacob, but the hands are the hands of Esau." And he did not recognize him, because his hands were hairy like his brother Esau's hands; so he blessed him. And he said, "Are you really my son Esau?" And he said, "I am." So he said, "Bring it to me, and I will eat of my son's game, that I may bless you." And he brought it to him, and he ate; he also brought him wine and he drank. Then his father Isaac said to him, "Please come close and kiss me, my son." So he came close and kissed him; and when he smelled the smell of his garments, he blessed him and said, "See, the smell of my son is like the smell of a field which the Lord has blessed; now may God give you of the dew of heaven, and of the fatness of the earth, and an abundance of grain and new wine; may peoples serve you, and nations bow down to you; be master of your brothers, and may your mother's sons bow down to you. Cursed be those who curse you, and blessed be those who bless you."

Now it came about, as soon as Isaac had finished blessing Jacob, and Jacob had hardly gone out from the presence of Isaac his father, that Esau his brother came in from his hunting.

Genesis 27:41-46 So Esau bore a grudge against Jacob because of the blessing with which his father had blessed him; and Esau said to himself, "The days of mourning for my father are near; then I will kill my brother Jacob." Now when the words of her elder son were reported to Rebekah, she sent and called her younger son Jacob, and said to him, "Behold your brother Esau is consoling himself concerning you, by planning to kill you. Now therefore, my son, obey my voice, and arise, flee to Haran, to my brother Laban! And stay with him a few days, until your brother's fury subsides, until your brother's anger against you subsides, and he forgets what you did to him. Then I shall send and get you from there. Why should I be bereaved of you both in one day?"

And Rebekah said to Isaac, "I am tired of living because of the daughters of Heth; if Jacob takes a wife from the daughters of Heth, like these, from the daughters of the land, what good will my life be to me?"

Rebekah became suspicious when she saw her elder son, Esau, go into Isaac's tent. *What were those two talking about?* she wondered. Driven by curiosity, she spied on the man whom many years ago she had considered to be a gift from God. Unthinkable!

Communications between Rebekah and Isaac had become poor. Their family unit had crumbled. It was parted into two miniworlds. One consisted of Jacob and herself, the other of Isaac and Esau. It appears that the children had driven them apart. The boys, though twins, were as different as night and day.

Hairy Esau was a rough man, both physically and in inward character. He liked to live outdoors, and had won his father's admiration because Isaac liked the meat Esau brought home from the hunt.

Jacob, the younger, was slightly built and cunning in character. He stayed at home and was his mother's favorite.

Having children should have drawn Isaac and Rebekah together, but, unfortunately, it seems to have driven them apart. Their marriage was marred by partiality.

Rebekah's love for Jacob was based on what God had said before the children were born. But on this day she had no time for contemplation. It was not a day to muse about the past. There were other things to consider. The future of her darling son, Jacob, was at stake.

Evidently it did not dawn on her that the future also concerned God's people, that it involved her husband and Esau. She neglected to consult God in her plan even though He had given distinct predictions about the future.

Rebekah, though 80 years old, had not lost her sharpness of intellect or quickness of action. She eavesdropped at her husband's door.

Isaac was over 100 years old and was preparing for death. The blessing which God had passed on to him through Abraham,[1] he now wanted to pass on—against the Word of God—to his older son. Such a solemn act between a father and his son was always celebrated with a meal.

Rebekah was alarmed. Something was going wrong. Hadn't God clearly predicted before the children were born that the elder would serve the younger?[2] This promise of God would be thwarted by what Isaac planned to do. This must not be allowed to happen.

Rebekah understood why God preferred Jacob. Esau had proven that he didn't take God's commandments seriously. He had sold the right which was his as the firstborn,[3] and which is holy in the sight of God.[4] Taking it very lightly, he had exchanged it for a plate of food.[5] He had also married heathen women. All this had caused much sorrow to his parents. And, although Jacob hadn't done the right thing when he had cunningly obtained the birthright, he had at least shown that he believed in it. His life was more God-centered than Esau's.

In the past, sorrow regarding their children had caused the parents to pray. Hadn't Rebekah's pregnancy been a result of Isaac's intercession? And hadn't Rebekah sought God when she realized to her surprise that the two children were fighting with one another even during her pregnancy?[6]

It is interesting to note that in both cases of praying only one parent is mentioned. Is this because of the brevity of the Scripture story? Or were they already getting into the habit of not sharing their thoughts with one another? Had the spry, intelligent Rebekah ever really loved the weak Isaac, who was much older? Had Isaac ever taken the trouble to win her love? Was their intense love for their sons an escape to replace the disunity of their own hearts? Or were they driven apart because they had attributed different values to the Word of God?

1. Genesis 17:1-8,21   3. Deuteronomy 21:15-17   5. Genesis 25:29-34
2. Romans 9:10-12   4. Exodus 13:2; Hebrews 12:16   6. Genesis 25:21-23

A marriage, which God compares with the bond between Christ and His Church, can only be happy if the partners function together. Although man and wife are equal before God,[7] they each have different responsibilities within the marriage bond. The man is the head.[8] He is responsible for his wife. He is to love her and to lead her according to the Word of God.[9] He is to honor her because she is the weaker of the two.[10] The wife must adapt herself to the husband. She is to obey him, to follow his leadership.

The secret of this relationship is Christ. The marriage is what God wants it to be when both partners subject themselves to one another because they honor Christ. Within this framework the partners fit into God's order of creation and experience the greatest possible personal fulfillment. When both comply with these conditions, the marriage functions as a happy and constructive unit. Then it provides a real home and protection for every member of the family and becomes the most important building stone of society.

The highest ambition for a woman having this perspective is to further the well-being of her husband: "She does him good and not evil all the days of her life."[11] If she manages her family, guided by this conviction, her husband and children will bless her and will consider themselves fortunate.[12]

Although Rebekah didn't have these requirements on a printed page, she must have known them, as Sarah did.[13] But, unfortunately, she didn't act on them. Isaac was not without blame either. Had he, as her husband, executed proper leadership in the way God expected?

Unfortunately, Rebekah took her lot in her own hands. This woman who once had sufficient faith to trust God for an unknown future now felt that she had to help Him out a bit. She lacked confidence that the eternal God was mighty enough to fulfill His promises to Jacob without human intervention. She did not take this opportunity to discuss the matter with her husband. An opportunity to grow closer together out of necessity, was bypassed. She decided, without hesitation, to deceive her husband and cheat Esau.

Jacob was not concerned about the act of the deception itself,

7. I Corinthians 11:11,12

8. I Corinthians 11:3,9

9. Ephesians 5:21-33

10. I Peter 3:7

11. Proverbs 31:12

12. Proverbs 31:28

13. I Peter 3:6

either. His only concern was that he might be discovered and bring a curse upon himself. Rebekah was prepared to do anything to further her cause. Had the gap between her and God so widened that she didn't fear His curse? She sounded reckless when she said, "I will take your curse upon me, my son . . . ."

The situation developed quickly. Before Esau entered his father's tent with his steaming meat dish, Jacob stole his blessing. Rebekah thought she had won, but she was wrong. She had lost. Her cunning action brought great sorrow upon Isaac. His name meant "laughing one," but he didn't have much to laugh about any more. And if Esau had once respected his mother, he would no longer.

Rebekah had also harmed Jacob, her favorite. With her help he had deceived his father by lying. He had slandered God's name when he told his father that God had given him his quick success in hunting. But that was not all. Jacob had developed into a master-deceiver. He could be as cunning as his mother.[15] That God blessed him in spite of all this was grace,[16] for Jacob certainly hadn't earned the blessing.

Jacob would later learn painfully that a deceiver will be deceived. First he would be deceived by his father-in-law,[17] then by his own children.[18] Also, how often would Jacob ask himself if he was really a man blessed by God, since his mother hadn't allowed God the chance to prove this? The stolen blessing was a doubtful possession.

It was also because of Rebekah's actions that Esau desired to kill Jacob later. This again led to deception. Jacob had to flee his parents' home. Rebekah's brother, Laban, supplied a good hiding place in Haran.

After she had arranged everything with Jacob, now a man over 40 years old, Rebekah went to Isaac. She said to her husband, "These foreign women are a burden. I would rather die than have Jacob marry one of them." What she said was true. Isaac and she had experienced much sorrow because of Esau's marriages. Yet she uttered no word of repentance for all she had done.

She had overestimated herself and made a false promise to Jacob that she would call for him when Esau's anger had turned away. She was unable to keep this promise because she did not live

14. Genesis 27:13
15. Genesis 30:37-43   17. Genesis 29:25
16. Genesis 31:11-13   18. Genesis 37:31-35

until Jacob's return. She saw her beloved son for the last time when he left to find a wife.[19] When he returned home 20 years later,[20] his father was still alive and Esau was reconciled with him, but Rebekah was dead.

Rebekah, like Sarah, was unable to foresee the far-reaching effects of her deeds. The hatred kindled in Esau's heart continued to future generations.[21] For many centuries the Edomites, Esau's descendants, would be the enemies of Israel. Herod the Great, the man who murdered the children in Bethlehem,[22] and his son Herod Antipas, the man who ridiculed Jesus at His trial,[23] were both Edomites, men from Idumea.

Rebekah, the woman who had been so carefully selected to be Isaac's wife, a woman chosen by God, had not fulfilled the promise expected of her. Her beginning was good, but her end was disappointing, because she couldn't wait upon God.[24] She took her lot in her own hands and didn't allow God to fight for her.[25] She forgot that those who believe do not need to make haste.[26] She neglected to give God a chance to show what He can and will do for those who wait upon Him.[27]

II. Rebekah takes her lot in her own hands
(Genesis 27:1-30, 41- 46)

Questions:
1. What characterized the Rebekah of the previous study?
2. What does Genesis 27 reveal about her faith?
3. What attitude characterized her as a mother?
4. What reasons could she have had for taking the future of Esau and Jacob in her own hands? (Romans 9:10-12)
5. Was it good for her to intervene as she did? Why or why not?
6. When you study Rebekah as a wife in light of Ephesians 5:21-33 and Proverbs 31:12, what conclusions can you draw?
7. You have probably learned several different things from the example of Rebekah. List them in the order of their importance and ask yourself what practical benefit they can have for you.

19. Genesis 28:1-4   22. Matthew 2:16   25. Deuteronomy 1:30; Exodus 14:13
20. Genesis 31:41   23. Luke 23:11   26. Isaiah 28:16
21. Ezekiel 25:12,13   24. Psalms 27:14; 37:34   27. Isaiah 64:4

4

"According to biblical thinking, two human beings who have shared the sexual act are never the same afterward. They can no longer act toward each other as if they had not had this experience. It makes out of those involved in it a couple bound to each other. It creates a one-flesh bond with all its implications."
Walter Trobisch*

Potiphar's wife, a woman swayed by sex

Genesis 39:1-20 Now Joseph had been taken down to Egypt; and Potiphar, an Egyptian officer of Pharaoh, the captain of the bodyguard, bought him from the Ishmaelites, who had taken him down there. And the Lord was with Joseph, so he became a successful man. And he was in the house of his master the Egyptian. Now his master saw that the Lord was with him and how the Lord caused all that he did to prosper in his hand. So Joseph found favor in his sight, and became his personal servant; and he made him overseer over his house, and all that he owned he put in his charge. And it came about that from the time he made him overseer in his house, and over all that he owned, the Lord blessed the Egyptian's house on account of Joseph; thus the Lord's blessing was upon all that he owned, in the house and in the field. So he left everything he owned in Joseph's charge; and with him around he did not concern himself with anything except the food which he ate. Now Joseph was handsome in form and appearance. And it came about after these events that his master's wife looked with desire at Joseph, and she said, "Lie with me." But he refused and said to his master's wife, "Behold, with me around, my master does not concern himself with anything in the house, and he has put all that he owns in my charge. There is no one greater in this

*Trobisch, Walter A. *I Married You,*
© 1971, Harper & Row, Publishers, New York, N.Y.

house than I, and he has withheld nothing from me except you, because you are his wife. How then could I do this great evil, and sin against God?" And it came about as she spoke to Joseph day after day, that he did not listen to her to lie beside her, or be with her. Now it happened one day that he went into the house to do his work, and none of the men of the household was there inside. And she caught him by his garment, saying, "Lie with me!" And he left his garment in her hand and fled, and went outside. When she saw that he had left his garment in her hand, and had fled outside, she called to the men of her household, and said to them, "See, he has brought in a Hebrew to us to make sport of us; he came in to me to lie with me, and I screamed. And it came about when he heard that I raised my voice and screamed, that he left his garment beside me and fled, and went outside." So she left his garment beside her until his master came home. Then she spoke to him with these words, "The Hebrew slave, whom you brought to us, came in to me to make sport of me; and it happened as I raised my voice and screamed, that he left his garment beside me and fled outside."

Now it came about when his master heard the words of his wife, which she spoke to him, saying, "This is what your slave did to me," that his anger burned. So Joseph's master took him and put him into the jail, the place where the king's prisoners were confined; and he was there in the jail.

I Thessalonians 4:3-5 For this is the will of God, your sanctification; that is, that you abstain from sexual immorality; that each of you know how to possess his own vessel in sanctification and honor, not in lustful passion, like the Gentiles who do not know God.

Potiphar's wife had everything. She had a husband who held a high-ranking position as an officer to Pharaoh.[1] She lived in a spacious and luxuriously furnished home. She wallowed in wealth, with food and clothing in abundance. She oversaw an extensive household staff, who provided her slightest wish. She was a spoiled woman.

As an Egyptian she also enjoyed greater liberty than many other women of her time. One could conclude that she would be very

---

1. Genesis 37

happy. But that conclusion would prove to be shortsighted, for the situation was really quite different.

It has been said that situations don't make a person; they reveal him. This is true of Potiphar's wife.

She appears in Scripture in connection with Joseph, the male head of her husband's household. Joseph, the son of Jacob and Rachel, was a strikingly handsome man when he arrived in the house of Potiphar after being sold into slavery by his brothers.

But Joseph's inner life was more remarkable than his good looks, for he had a close walk with God. Several times God had revealed Joseph's future to him in dreams. That was one reason his brothers had been jealous of him. They had felt he looked upon them with disdain. When they had further realized that their father favored Joseph, their fury reached its limit. They got rid of him by selling him to passing merchants.

It soon became very clear that God was with Joseph, however, for wherever Joseph went, the blessing of God followed. Thus, Potiphar's house was blessed—because of Joseph. A relationship of mutual appreciation and respect grew up between Joseph and his master. Consequently, Joseph's responsibilities increased until, finally, he was in charge of the entire household.

Potiphar's wife, who at first glance seemed to possess everything a woman could desire, was inwardly empty, a woman without purpose. She had too much time on her hands. She was married to a man to whom work meant everything. While the Bible doesn't mention any children, if there had been any, they would have most certainly been cared for by a nurse.

Perhaps her feelings were hurt because her husband did not give her the attention she desired. An empty life searches for fulfillment and an empty heart craves satisfaction. Potiphar's wife ultimately gave expression to desires which were in her heart.

Didn't she realize that it was Joseph's inner character of beauty, righteousness and fidelity that was attractive, not just his physical appearance? Couldn't she understand that the special thing about him was his close walk with God?

Evidently not, for she humiliated herself and Joseph, not once, but repeatedly. She imposed herself and her body upon him. She

Paul later earnestly warned against sin controlling one's life.[2] The body is not for fornication, but for the Lord (I Corinthians 6:13b). God expects the human body to function as His temple (I Corinthians 6:19).

expected to find satisfaction in sex alone. She didn't know that the sensation she craved would only produce passion, an emotional excitement that would consume her if the act was not grounded in love and the security of marriage.

In creation God said, "For this cause a man shall leave his father and his mother, and shall cleave to his wife; and they shall become one flesh."[3] So sexuality has been included by God forever in the warmth, security and love of marriage. This is clear by His order—the becoming of one flesh was to be a result of love. The decision to leave one's parents—starting a household—provides the proper environment for the culmination of sexual love. Without these prerequisites sex is a lust which consumes, which can degrade a human being to a low animal level. This results in self-accusation, loneliness and shame. It creates a still greater loneliness, for the craving for more sensual passion has been established. Finally utter desolation results. It becomes a vicious cycle of misery.

The trouble ahead for Potiphar's wife could not be overlooked, and she certainly could not find a solution to her problems in sex. Sexuality, used in this manner, creates its own hell.

Joseph immediately put the temptation into proper perspective. He did not minimize it, but called it what it

God later gave a law to His people through Moses which requires that adultery be punished by death (Deuteronomy 22:13,14, 20-22). God doesn't want to deny man pleasure; He desires the best and greatest happiness for him. He wants to protect him from the destruction which always accompanies immorality. God cannot allow the greatest earthly gift He has given to be degraded and disgraced.

was—sin. He spoke of the great respect he felt toward her husband. But his greatest concern was God. "How can I do this evil, and sin against God?" he asked. Joseph was right; fornication and adultery are sins in the sight of God. Every act of sexual intercourse outside marriage is a sin which God abhors.

Immorality is one of the deadly weapons which comes straight from hell and which destroys the person who indulges in it. Joseph knew this well because he walked with God. He knew what displeased the Creator.

2. Romans 6:12
3. Genesis 2:24

"The one who commits adultery with a woman is lacking sense; he who would destroy himself does it. Wounds and disgrace he will find, and his reproach will not be blotted out."[4] While Solomon wrote these words many years later, Joseph understood and applied this principle in the situation with Potiphar's wife.

The fact that Potiphar's wife didn't know the God of Israel was no excuse. She, like everyone, was innately a moral person. She was trespassing a law of life that God gave to mankind in creation.[5] She proved this when she twisted the truth after Joseph had rejected her. She accused *him* of the immorality she had intended to commit herself! Joseph's hasty flight, which give proof to his purity of character, exposed her even more and twisted her mind. Being his superior, she decided, without any scruples, to ruin his career and stain his good name.

This ushered in a difficult time for Joseph—a stay of many years in prison. He undoubtedly felt very hurt by the dishonest accusations. He probably felt forsaken, too, since Potiphar apparently did not investigate the situation. Evidently, however, Potiphar didn't believe his wife or he would have certainly had Joseph put to death.

Joseph didn't complain. To his joy he found that even prison walls could not exclude God. God was still with him, as He had been in Potiphar's house. Again Joseph was a blessing to those around him. He was finally rewarded for his loyalty to God and his master, and given rule over all of Egypt. He was second in command to Pharaoh, the ruler of Egypt. He became Zaphenath-paaneah, the protector of the people. Eventually he was able to save the brothers who betrayed him when they were threatened by starvation.

Joseph was not the loser.

Potiphar's wife was.

Nothing more is heard about her—not because of the magnitude of her sin, but because she showed no sorrow and asked no forgiveness. She appeared to desire no knowledge of God, even though He was so willing to give her joy and satisfaction in life that He had touched her life through the person of Joseph.

She could have found victory over her sexual desires if she had recognized them as sin in time. She could even have regained

4. Proverbs 6:32,33
5. Romans 2:14,15

control of her mind and body after Joseph's first rejection of her. She could have asked Joseph about the God who was governing his life. She could have filled her idle hours more profitably.

Idleness became the parent of her vice, for she acted carelessly with one of life's most precious gifts—time. She spent it uselessly. Idleness became the soil that nourished her sinful thoughts. Only after she succumbed to her evil thoughts was she then confronted by the desire to sin in deed. Since deeds are the fruit of thoughts, her thoughts were the source of her downfall. A person becomes what he or she thinks. The temptation of Potiphar's wife was not unusual. Millions of people today are being tempted in the same manner, because Satan continually goes about like a roaring lion, seeking someone to devour.[6] He will never change his character.

Potiphar's wife allowed her temptation to grow into sin because she did not curb her desires, but rather allowed them to entice and draw her into an actual sin.[7] She had no desire to correct herself.

She had the time, the intelligence and the potential to use her life positively, but failed. Therefore, no good word can be said about her. It is tragic that she lived without having left behind any positive impression.

Potiphar's wife, a woman swayed by sex
(Genesis 39:1-20; I Thessalonians 4:3-5)

Questions:
1. In a few sentences record what the Bible says about Potiphar's wife.
2. What words did Joseph use to put her immoral proposal in the proper perspective?

6. I Peter 5:8
7. James 1:14,15

3. Study the law of Moses regarding God's thoughts about sexual relations between a man and a woman who are not married. (Deuteronomy 22:13,14,20-22). What strikes you?
4. The wife of Potiphar didn't know God's laws. Why was her ignorance no excuse? (Remember Romans 2:14,15.)
5. For whom was the human body created and why? (I Corinthians 6:13b,19,20)
6. Compare this story with the warning in I Thessalonians 4:3-5. What attitude does God want people to have in regard to their bodies?

*"Search me, O God, and know my heart; test my
thoughts. Point out anything You find in
me that makes You sad, and lead me along the path
of everlasting life."* A prayer of David*

Miriam,
a leader who overestimated herself

Exodus 15:19-21 For the horses of Pharaoh with his chariots and
his horsemen went into the sea, and the Lord brought back the
waters of the sea on them; but the sons of Israel walked on dry land
through the midst of the sea. And Miriam the prophetess, Aaron's
sister, took the timbrel in her hand, and all the women went out after
her with timbrels and with dancing. And Miriam answered them,
"Sing to the Lord, for He is highly exalted; the horse and his rider He
has hurled into the sea."

Numbers 12:1-15 Then Miriam and Aaron spoke against Moses
because of the Cushite woman whom he had married (for he had
married a Cushite woman); and they said, "Has the Lord indeed
spoken only through Moses? Has He not spoken through us as
well?" And the Lord heard it. (Now the man Moses was very
humble, more than any man who was on the face of the earth.) And
suddenly the Lord said to Moses and Aaron and to Miriam, "You
three come out to the tent of meeting." So the three of them came
out. Then the Lord came down in a pillar of cloud and stood at the
doorway of the tent, and He called Aaron and Miriam. When they
had both come forward, He said, "Hear now My words: If there is a
prophet among you, I the Lord shall make Myself known to him in a

*Psalm 139:23,24. Taylor, Kenneth N. *The Living Bible,*
© 1971, Tyndale House Publishers, Wheaton, Illinois.

vision. I shall speak with him in a dream. Not so, with My servant Moses, He is faithful in all My household; with him I speak mouth to mouth, even openly, and not in dark sayings, and he beholds the form of the Lord. Why then were you not afraid to speak against My servant, against Moses?"

So the anger of the Lord burned against them and He departed. But when the cloud had withdrawn from over the tent, behold, Miriam was leprous, as white as snow. As Aaron turned toward Miriam, behold, she was leprous. Then Aaron said to Moses, "Oh, my lord, I beg you, do not account this sin to us, in which we have acted foolishly and in which we have sinned. Oh do not let her be like one dead, whose flesh is half eaten away when he comes from his mother's womb!" And Moses cried out to the Lord, saying, "Oh God, heal her, I pray!" But the Lord said to Moses, "If her father had but spit in her face, would she not bear her shame for seven days? Let her be shut up for seven days outside the camp, and afterward she may be received again." So Miriam was shut up outside the camp for seven days, and the people did not move on until Miriam was received again.

Numbers 20:1 Then the sons of Israel, the whole congregation, came to the wilderness of Zin in the first month; and the people stayed at Kadesh. Now Miriam died there and was buried there.

Miriam had been an intelligent child. Her mother had readily entrusted her with an assignment of such importance that the life of her younger brother was dependent upon her success. She completed her task with courage and tact, bringing her mother, a Hebrew woman, and an Egyptian princess in contact with each other. Thus her brother was rescued, benefiting both their family and God's people.[1] The child was Moses, mediator of the old covenant, the prophet who spoke face to face with God.

As an adult, Miriam was a woman of stature. Her character had been formed in a family where faith was a daily reality. Her parents had the courage, the love and the ingenuity to defy the commands of a tyrannical king in order to save the life of their youngest son. The family of Amram and Jochebed was unique in Israel's existence, for it brought forth three great leaders—Moses, Aaron

1. Exodus 2:1-10

and Miriam—who all served the nation at the same time.

"I brought you up from the land of Egypt, and ransomed you from the house of slavery, and I sent before you Moses, Aaron, and Miriam," God later declared through the prophet Micah.[2] When Moses led his troublesome people out of Egypt to Canaan, he was assisted by his brother Aaron, the high priest, and his sister Miriam, the prophetess.

She was not just a tagalong sister. She was his colaborer, with leadership responsibilities. Miriam, an unmarried woman, was called by God to an exceptional task. She had the privilege of being the first female prophet—a spokeswoman for God.

In deeds and words she proclaimed the greatness of God. Her life was totally centered on loving God and His people. Her gifts and interests were too great to be used exclusively for the small family circle. Israel had many wives and mothers, but only one Miriam. God entrusted her with a high position. An entire nation was dependent upon her. She received supreme satisfaction in life, as she dedicated herself wholly to the task.

She was nearing the age of one hundred when the miracle of the Red Sea astounded the masses. The water that brought salvation to God's people confirmed the fall of His enemies. "I will sing to the Lord, for He has triumphed gloriously," cried Moses afterward; "He has drowned the horse and rider in the sea."[3] After the men had started the joyous singing, the women continued it. From that day forth, Israel would always sing about exceptional victories because of Miriam. She was first in line—energetic and youthful in spirit in spite of her age. With timbrel in her hand, she took over the song from Moses. She encouraged the women to dance to the honor of God while shouting for joy, ". . . sing to the Lord, for He has triumphed gloriously."

Miriam was a born leader. The women readily followed her. And although they could not foresee the future, their singing would become an endless source of support to the women during their long wilderness wanderings. One walks better when singing and there is less worry. There was no way for her to know how often it was going to be necessary to encourage one another with the faithfulness of God. The journey was long because of the

2. Micah 6:4
3. Exodus 15:1

disobedience of the people. But they gained new courage when singing, "The horse and rider He has drowned in the sea." However, self-conceit was becoming fatal to Miriam.

She was a strong woman. Leadership came easily to her. And, as is often the case, this very strength became a weakness. It has been said that circumstances reveal the inner person. The circumstance that revealed Miriam's inner character was Moses' second marriage, this time to an Ethiopian.

It is understandable that Miriam found this difficult. It was strange that Moses, a man of God, would again marry a woman from another nation. Or was she simply reacting to the presence of another woman in the life of Moses, especially since she was unmarried herself? Was she indignant because he was satisfied with a foreign woman, while countless Israelite women would have been more suitable? These questions are not answered in the Scriptures.

Moses, the great leader of the Israelites, was Miriam's younger brother, and she was worried about him. She was concerned about how the results of this marriage might affect the people. The marriage took place in a period of history when relatives usually decided upon matters of marriage. Looking at her concern from this standpoint, it would seem to be a proper spiritual reaction from a mature woman. But it was far from that.

Miriam, who had ascended to the highest post ever held by a woman, and who was named by God in the same breath as the two great male leaders, had simply surpassed her boundaries. She overestimated herself. She considered herself to be on the same level as Moses. And in her pride she undermined his authority. "Was he, indeed, the leader of the three of them?" she asked. "Weren't she and Aaron his equals?"

Miriam was not motivated by concern for the well-being of the people or for Moses, but by jealousy. Aaron, the most pliable of the three, could not resist his domineering sister, so he went along with her. Together Miriam and Aaron tried to usurp Moses' authority. In doing this, they endangered the unity and future of the entire nation. Moreover, they attempted to thwart the direct revelation of God. Instead of thinking about the well-being of everyone concerned, they thought only selfishly.[4]

4. Philippians 2:3,4

God created man to give himself to others. When a person does this he experiences the greatest happiness. It enriches and widens his horizons. But his life becomes poor and limited when he selfishly desires only to receive—when he himself is in the center of his thinking.

Moses remained calm. He showed no desire to defend himself. There was, however, another who defended Moses' rights, and this became a frightful experience for Miriam and Aaron. For God in heaven heard, knew and saw what was happening on earth. He took immediate steps to stop the rebellion against Moses' leadership and to punish the guilty ones.

Shattered and with shaky knees, Aaron and Miriam appeared before God. They heard how He judged the situation. Moses, they heard, was not only the undisputed leader, he was also given a position higher than all the prophets.

It was clear that God had chosen Moses to be the mediator between Himself and His people. He respected Moses so highly that He didn't speak to him through vague riddles and obscure dreams. Instead, He spoke to Moses as a man speaks to his friends[5]—openly, plainly.

Miriam and Aaron had attacked a man highly respected by God. When He in His godly justice and authority called them to account, they had no excuse. Ultimately they had not harmed Moses, but themselves. Moses, the God-appointed mediator, was a type of the Saviour to come. To reject Moses was, in fact, to reject the Messiah. This was what made the situation so serious.

When God left them in His anger, Miriam had become a leper. It was the most dreaded of diseases, for it sapped the strength of the person who had it. It degraded him with a walking death. And God had stained her with the curse of leprosy.

The woman who for years had gone ahead of the crowd singing, who had challenged the other women to sing praises to God, had been expelled from the ranks of leadership. Her voice, which had once so melodiously praised God, now shouted a hoarse "unclean, unclean," when anyone came within her reach. The members of her body would gradually become more and more hideous, until they finally dropped off. She would go through life crippled and lonely until her death.

5. Exodus 33:11

Miriam had to experience very painfully how great her sin was in the eyes of God. The shame of her deed could be compared to a father spitting in the face of his child publicly. Therefore, she had to undergo her punishment publicly, so that everyone could see how God punished people who thought too highly of themselves.[6] Miriam, the brave, active woman, found no words to answer His curse.

Aaron regained his composure first and indicated that he had accepted the correction. He said to Moses, "Oh, my lord"—he did not call him "brother," but "lord," thus recognizing Moses' leadership. "Don't punish us for being foolish and sinning." Aaron identified himself completely with Miriam's sin. Then it was not he, the high priest, but Moses who entreated God for her healing. Moses didn't indicate that he approved of God's judgment nor did he rebuke Miriam and Aaron. He simply prayed to God, and his prayer reduced Miriam's sentence from one of lifelong suffering to only seven days.

Miriam's attitude had brought harm not only to herself but also to her people. Their journey had been delayed because of her sin. The entire nation was kept from moving forward until Miriam was among them again. The seven days she spent as an outcast must have given Miriam much food for thought. Did she then understand that God Himself appoints His leaders?—that in His godly order He entrusts leadership to those who are humble enough to be willing to serve?[7] Had she come out a better person? Had she been purified?

The Bible doesn't record any further rebellion. Had the experience destroyed Miriam's strength and usefulness? Did she lose her gift of prophecy? The Bible doesn't say, but it does state that she died before her people entered the promised land.

Miriam was a woman at the top. It was an exceptional position, a commission which had been entrusted to her by God. Miriam's story offered a wonderful challenge as long as she used her position to honor God. A person who does this can hardly go wrong. However, Miriam gradually shifted away from God's control in her life to self control. This no doubt occurred so subtly that she didn't realize the change was taking place. Perhaps if she had searched her heart honestly in time, she could have prevented

6. Romans 12:3
7. Luke 22:24-27; I Peter 5:5,6

God's judgment.[8] Perhaps then she would not have overstepped her boundaries by overestimating herself.

Miriam, a leader who overestimated herself
(Exodus 15:19-21; Numbers 12:1-15; 20:1)
Questions:
1. What did you discover concerning Miriam's personality and character?
2. What exceptional place did she have among her people? (Micah 6:4)
3. How did she behave when authority was placed over her, and by what did she prove that she overestimated herself?
4. What do Philippians 2:3,4 and Romans 12:3 teach about criticism and overestimating oneself?
5. What were the results of her sin? For herself and for others?
6. Formulate what you have learned from her example. How can this influence your own life favorably?

8. I Corinthians 11:31

6

"An innkeeper's bill from Roman days:
Wine and bread, 1 ace.
Hot meal, 2 ace.
Hay for mule, 2 ace.
One girl, 8 ace."
P.S. There is no separate cost for the bed;
that was included with the last item.*

Rahab,
a harlot in the gallery of the heroes of faith

Joshua 2:1-21 Then Joshua the son of Nun sent two men as spies secretly from Shittim, saying, "Go, view the land, especially Jericho." So they went and came into the house of a harlot whose name was Rahab, and lodged there. And it was told the king of Jericho, saying, "Behold, men from the sons of Israel have come here tonight to search out the land." And the king of Jericho sent word to Rahab, saying, "Bring out the men who have come to you, who have entered your house, for they have come to search out all the land." But the woman had taken the two men and hidden them, and she said, "Yes, the men came to me, but I did not know where they were from. And it came about when it was time to shut the gate, at dark, that the men went out; I do not know where the men went. Pursue them quickly, for you will overtake them." But she had brought them up to the roof and hidden them in the stalks of flax which she had laid in order on the roof. So the men pursued them on the road to the Jordan to the fords; and as soon as those who were pursuing them had gone out, they shut the gate.

Now before they lay down, she came up to them on the roof, and said to the men, "I know that the Lord has given you the land, and that the terror of you has fallen on us, and that all the inhabitants of the land have melted away before you. For we have heard how the

---

Aus dem Leben der Antike (From the Life of the Antiques),
Birt. Quoted by D. J. Baarslag in *Baals en Burchten (Baals and Fortresses).* Bosch & Keuning, Baarn. The Netherlands.

Lord dried up the water of the Red Sea before you when you came out of Egypt, and what you did to the two kings of the Amorites who were beyond the Jordan, to Sihon and Og, whom you utterly destroyed. And when we heard it, our hearts melted and no courage remained in any man any longer because of you; for the Lord your God, He is God in heaven above and on earth beneath. Now therefore, please swear to me by the Lord, since I have dealt kindly with you, that you also will deal kindly with my father's household, and give me a pledge of truth, and spare my father and my mother and my brothers and my sisters, with all who belong to them, and deliver our lives from death." So the men said to her, "Our life for yours if you do not tell this business of ours; and it shall come about when the Lord gives us the land that we will deal kindly and faithfully with you."

Then she let them down by a rope through the window, for her house was on the city wall, so that she was living on the wall. And she said to them, "Go to the hill country, lest the pursuers happen upon you, and hide yourselves there for three days, until the pursuers return. Then afterward you may go on your way." And the men said to her, "We shall be free from this oath to you which you have made us swear, unless, when we come into the land, you tie this cord of scarlet thread in the window through which you let us down, and gather to yourself into the house your father and your mother and your brothers and all your father's household. And it shall come about that anyone who goes out of the doors of your house into the street, his blood shall be on his own head, and we shall be free; but anyone who is with you in the house, his blood shall be on our head, if a hand is laid on him. But if you tell this business of ours, then we shall be free from the oath which you have made us swear." And she said, "According to your words, so be it." So she sent them away, and they departed; and she tied the scarlet cord in the window.

Joshua 6:22-25 And Joshua said to the two men who had spied out the land, "Go into the harlot's house and bring the woman and all she has out of there, as you have sworn to her." So the young men who were spies went in and brought out Rahab and her father and her mother and her brothers and all she had; they also brought out all her relatives, and placed them outside the camp of Israel. And they burned the city with fire, and all that was in it. Only the silver and gold and articles of bronze and iron, they put into the treasury of the house of the Lord. However, Rahab the harlot and her father's household and all she had, Joshua spared; and she has lived in the midst of Israel to this day, for she hid the messengers whom Joshua sent to spy out Jericho.

The Bible is an honest book which states facts as they are—candidly. Rahab, the Bible says, was a harlot, a woman who sold her body for money. People have tried to cover up this sad fact, stating that she was an innkeeper. This was probably true, but the fact remains that she was a woman of corrupted morals.

In those days the innkeepers were women, never men. It is interesting to note that in the written bills of later Roman times an amount was annotated for the meal and the girl, but the cost of the bed was not mentioned—it apparently was included with the price of the girl. She provided an "extra service" by offering her body, and this was included in the bill.

Since Rahab was in a position to lodge guests, it was natural for Joshua's spies to go to her place. Jericho was a small town, and Rahab's inn was probably the only place to sleep.

Did Rahab suspect that these foreigners—decent men without hidden motives—were Israelites? The Bible doesn't say. But it does say that counterespionage was launched immediately. The king heard that Jewish scouts were in the city and called for their immediate capture.

Meanwhile, Rahab had become aware of the true identity of her guests and had already hidden them on her roof under stacks of flax. Since it was harvest time and the walled city was small, the inhabitants of the tiny houses on the narrow streets had to use every available inch of space for storage. An open roof was the least ideal spot to hide people since even from a distance, others could see everything that went on there. But Rahab's house was different. It was built on the double city wall and was situated higher than any other house, so no curious eyes could watch what went on there. The spies would be safe, but only for a short time.

Rahab misled the king's messengers. While they searched the surrounding countryside carefully, she talked with the hidden spies. She told them she was aware that God had given them the land and that the inhabitants of her land were fearful of them because of the miracle of the parting of the Red Sea.[1] She was well aware of what God had done for His people. She told them that the men had lost courage to face the Israelites because of their God.

She proved to be a wise woman who acted in the light of proper information. She used discretion in talking about them and shrewdness in hiding them. She felt that one good turn deserved another, "Since I have saved your lives, will you in turn save mine and that of my relatives?"

Yet she naturally expressed concern about herself while at the same time expressing faith in the God of Israel. She believed that He fought for His people and that He was going to give them this land. She also believed that because of this God's power, her people didn't have the slightest chance of keeping the Israelites outside the city walls. She acted upon this faith.

She asked for a sign that they would save her when their armies returned to take the city. They told her to put a scarlet cord on her window and no one would be harmed in her household.

Some Bible commentators say that this scarlet ribbon represented Rahab's immoral occupation. It was her "red light," and therefore, would cause no suspicion. Nobody would suspect it to be a sign of espionage. This may or may not have been true, but it was certainly a clear indication of an agreement between the two parties.

Rahab did not delay. The men had hardly left when she bound the red ribbon at her window. She wanted to be absolutely certain that her house was easily distinguishable from all the others.

God likes it when people—even unbelievers—take their business seriously. Jesus proved this later when He told His disciples, that the sons of this world are wiser in their own generation than the sons of light.[2]

A week later the miracle of the Red Sea repeated itself. Again deep water was parted. The Israelites walked with dry feet through the river Jordan, which at that time was high above its banks. A few days later Rahab saw a throng of Israelites walking around the city in silent procession. The city gates were closed. No Jew could come in; no Canaanite could get out. This state of affairs continued for six days.

---

1. Exodus 14:26-30
2. Luke 16:8b

Now and then she reassured herself that the red ribbon was definitely visible, for her life would soon depend upon its being seen.

On the seventh day, the Israelites again walked silently around and around the city. Their faces were solemn. The tension on both sides of the wall was becoming unbearable. Inside, the people viewed the future with eyes full of horror and fear—except in one house. In Rahab's home there was hope and trust. She had made a covenant with the people of God and, therefore, with God Himself.

Then seven priests with seven trumpets of rams' horns encompassed the city blowing their horns, and the people, on Joshua's command, began to shout. Then the unbelievable happened. The earth began to tremble. Walls which had safeguarded the city for years crumbled and fell apart, leaving the city unprotected.

The writer of Hebrews later said faith had caused the walls to fall.[3] And that very same faith had caused a part of the wall to remain erect—the wall where Rahab's house stood.

Both parties had fulfilled their part of the agreement. Rahab had done her part and God had rewarded her faith. Her faith in the victory of the God of Israel was so strong that she was able to convince her relatives to come and stay with her. Every one of them was spared.

Rahab's life portrait was marred because of the dishonoring stain of immorality. Yet it was brightened with an example of glistening faith—her faith was strong enough for her to act. This was necessary, says James, who also writes of her;[4] for if faith cannot stand the test of use, then it is useless—dead. Inner faith can only be recognized by outward deeds.

One definition of faith is that it is a fixed and profound trust in God and His Word. Rahab had this kind of faith. Therefore, God took her tarnished portrait, cleansed it and hung it next to Sarah in the gallery of the heroes of faith. These two women are the only two females in a long list of men.

Rahab, like Sarah, a heroine of faith? Yes. For God is no respecter of persons. There are no impossible cases with Him. He justifies the ungodly. But Rahab's story didn't end there. The

3. Hebrews 11:30,31
4. James 2:25

conquest of Jericho only marked the beginning, for she had now found God. Her life began to blossom. There was no further longing for her former occupation; instead, she became an honorable housewife. She, a heathen woman, lived among the Jewish people, married the Israelite Salmon, and had a child. If we were to evaluate her effectiveness as a mother by her sympathetic and wise son, Boaz, the husband of Ruth, then she did very well indeed, for Ruth becomes the great-grandmother of King David.[5] Rahab became a mother in the lineage of Jesus Christ, the Messiah, a privilege every Jewish woman would envy.

By faith—

Rahab, a harlot in the gallery of the heroes of faith
(Joshua 2:1-21; 6:22-25)

Questions:
1. Describe briefly what you have learned about Rahab.
2. What strikes you about her knowledge of the God of Israel?
3. What was Rahab's attitude as a result of her knowledge of God? (Read also James 2:25.)
4. Why, according to Hebrews 11:31, didn't she perish with those who were disobedient? Mention various things which proved her faith.
5. What impact did her faith have on her relatives and herself?
6. What do you consider the most remarkable thing you have learned about Rahab? How are you going to apply this to your life?

5. Matthew 1:5 and the Book of Ruth

7

"Leading health authorities have determined that the deeper cause of much illness is in the emotional reactions to life. Prolonged bitter hatred can damage the brain, and can cause heart disorders, high blood pressure and acute indigestion—all severe enough to kill a person."
Robert D. Foster*

Peninnah, a woman conquered by jealousy

I Samuel 1:1-8 Now there was a certain man from Ramathaim-zophim from the hill country of Ephraim, and his name was Elkanah the son of Jeroham, the son of Elihu, the son of Tohu, the son of Zuph, an Ephraimite. And he had two wives: the name of one was Hannah and the name of the other Peninnah; and Peninnah had children, but Hannah had no children. Now this man would go up from his city yearly to worship and to sacrifice to the Lord of hosts in Shiloh. And the two sons of Eli, Hophni and Phinehas were priests to the Lord there. And when the day came that Elkanah sacrificed, he would give portions to Peninnah his wife and to all her sons and her daughters; but to Hannah he would give a double portion, for he loved Hannah, but the Lord had closed her womb. Her rival, however, would provoke her bitterly to irritate her, because the Lord had closed her womb. And it happened year after year, as often as she went up to the house of the Lord, she would provoke her, so she wept and would not eat. Then Elkanah her husband said to her, "Hannah, why do you weep and why do you not eat and why is your heart sad? Am I not better to you than ten sons?"

Studies in Christian Living, Book 4, "Character of the Christian,"
© 1964, The Navigators, Colorado Springs, Colorado.

Proverbs 6:24 To keep you from the evil woman, from the smooth tongue of the adulteress.

Proverbs 14:30 A tranquil heart is life to the body, but passion is rottenness to the bones.

Proverbs 27:4 Wrath is fierce and anger is a flood, but who can stand before jealousy?

Peninnah lived in a time of decline. Israel had arrived at one of the darkest points in her history. After Moses and Joshua had ruled the nation so capably, the time of the judges arrived.

God Himself wanted to rule. However, the people were little interested in God and they increasingly turned toward serving idols. Thus theocratic rule failed.

The decline resulted in anarchy. The laws of the government were no longer obeyed. Every man was doing what was right in his own eyes.[1] The spiritual climate was no better than the political and social. The wrath of God was accumulating upon the head of Eli, the head priest, because he tolerated the bad behavior of his sons, Hophni and Phinehas.

Eli saw that they were eating the best of the sacrifices offered to God by the people. He knew that they degraded the tabernacle by engaging in sexual misbehavior. Yet he didn't rebuke them.[2]

The judgment of God was at hand. The house of Eli had lost its influence and the nation was about to be besieged by its enemy, the Philistines.

But even more dreadful than this was that God hardly spoke during these days. There was little communication between Him and His people.[3]

Peninnah lived during this period. Elkanah, her husband, had two wives. God meant for each man to have only one wife and each woman to have only one husband.[4] But, since people fell away from His ideal, He provided for these exceptions, mainly to protect the firstborn son.[5]

As Elkanah experienced, anyone who deviates from God's plans brings difficulty upon himself and others. The atmosphere in his home was unbearable. The fact that Peninnah had children while

1. Judges 21:25
2. I Samuel 2:12-33   4. Genesis 2:18; Matthew 19:4-6; I Corinthians 7:2
3. I Samuel 3:1b   5. Deuteronomy 21:15-17

his other wife, Hannah, did not, just added fuel to the conflict.

At least the form of religion had its proper place in Elkanah's family. But although every member paid his religious tributes, God was not real to Peninnah. She was discontented. She was not grateful to Him for her children and the other good things she possessed. Her life was paralyzed by a lack of thankfulness. It must not have dawned on her that God desired other tributes; for example, loving others. She had everything a Jewish woman could desire, because she had many children. This was generally a proof of God's favor. She would continue to live in the future through the lives of her children long after she was dead.

On the other hand, Elkanah's other wife was heavily burdened by her childlessness. Hannah was not affected by the spirit of the times in which she lived. Because God was central in her thoughts, her deeds were inspired by faith. She was attractive and mild-mannered. Elkanah saw the difference between the two women clearly. He could not help but prefer Hannah over Peninnah.

But Peninnah was not inspired by Hannah's example. In fact, her response was just the opposite. She exalted herself over Hannah because she had given birth to children—many children. The fact that God was the One who had made it possible for her to have them didn't enter her mind.

Peninnah was jealous of Hannah. She provoked her incessantly, especially when the Jewish holidays arrived. These days caused Hannah extra pain anyway because they were family celebrations, during which the nation moved by families to the house of God in Shiloh. It seemed Peninnah was even more bitter toward Hannah during these days.

Peninnah had allowed her bitterness to take root in her heart.[6] And since she hadn't guarded her heart,[7] her life had become poisoned with envy. This envy stemmed from rivalry, selfishness and a lack of humility. Envy looks only after its own interests, not those of others. The Bible warns strongly against it.[8] Envy is not one of those small character weaknesses that God will allow a man to live with. He puts it in a list of sins which society considers to be far greater: adultery, idolatry, witchcraft, etc.[9]

"Jealousy is the rage of a man," wrote Solomon. It is like a fire. If not quenched rapidly it cannot be stopped, because it affects

---

6. Hebrews 12:15   8. Philippians 2:3,4
7. Proverbs 4:23   9. Galatians 5:19-21

other parts of the body. This is especially true of the tongue.[10] Peninnah is an example of how a person can use her tongue to vent her jealousy. Being one of the smallest members of the body, the tongue can cause a blazing flame which can destroy entire lives.[11] No wonder that in such a case the Bible says a person misusing the tongue is "set on fire by hell."[12]

Jealousy devours a person because it stems from Satan. In fact, it destroyed Satan himself. He envied God. In his pride he wanted to be like Him, and this caused his downfall.[13] Therefore, Satan is happy every time a human falls into this snare he has prepared. Often he has great success, for people are jealous by nature. It is ironic that men can allow the same member, the tongue, which they use to talk to God and to honor Him, to be inspired by Satan.

Jealousy begins in the mind. If it is not arrested in time and brought to God,[14] it ruins one's thought life and hinders interpersonal relationships. It is also subtle. It is a far greater danger to the person who harbors it than it is to the person toward whom it is directed. Like a boomerang, it returns to the envious person. Peninnah experienced this. She did not manage to solve her problems, even while the solution was within her grasp. All she needed to do was observe and follow the example of Hannah's faith.

Peninnah, a woman conquered by jealousy
(I Samuel 1:1-8; Proverbs 6:24; 14:30; 27:4)

Questions:
1. What remarkable words do you read in the account of Peninnah's behavior toward Hannah?
2. Being a Jewish woman with children, Peninnah was privileged above the childless Hannah. Why did she treat Hannah the way she did?
3. How are envy and the other sins mentioned in Galatians 5:19-21 labeled? What strikes you as you compare this vice with the others listed there?

10. Romans 3:14

11. James 3:16

12. James 3:2-8

13. Isaiah 14:13-15

14. II Corinthians 10:5

4. Consider Peninnah's life in light of Proverbs 4:23 and II Corinthians 10:5. What conclusions do you draw?
5. What can you learn about her life when you consider it in light of James 3:2-8?
6. Are there things in your life you would want to correct after studying Peninnah? Pray about this, then decide how you can start doing it.

8

"The great people of the earth today are the people who pray. I do not mean those who talk about prayer; nor those who can explain about prayer; but I mean those people who take time and pray. They have not time. It must be taken from something else. This something else is important, very important and pressing, but still less important and less pressing than prayer." S. D. Gordon*

Hannah, a woman who believed in prayer

I Samuel 1:9-28 Then Hannah rose after eating and drinking in Shiloh. Now Eli the priest was sitting on the seat by the doorpost of the temple of the Lord. And she, greatly distressed, prayed to the Lord and wept bitterly. And she made a vow and said, "O Lord of hosts, if Thou wilt indeed look on the affliction of Thy maidservant and remember me, and not forget Thy maidservant, but wilt give Thy maidservant a son, then I will give him to the Lord all the days of his life, and a razor shall never come on his head."

Now it came about, as she continued praying before the Lord, that Eli was watching her mouth. As for Hannah, she was speaking in her heart, only her lips were moving, but her voice was not heard. So Eli thought she was drunk. Then Eli said to her, "How long will you make yourself drunk? Put away your wine from you." But Hannah answered and said, "No, my lord, I am a woman oppressed in spirit; I have drunk neither wine nor strong drink, but I have poured out my soul before the Lord. Do not consider your maidservant as a worthless woman; for I have spoken until now out of my great concern and provocation." Then Eli answered and said, "Go in peace; and may the God of Israel grant your petition that you have asked of Him." And she said, "Let your maidservant find favor

Design for Discipleship, Book 2, "The Spirit-filled Christian," © 1973, The Navigators, Colorado Springs, Colorado.

in your sight." So the woman went her way and ate, and her face was no longer sad.

Then they arose early in the morning and worshipped before the Lord, and returned again to their house in Ramah. And Elkanah had relations with Hannah his wife, and the Lord remembered her. And it came about in due time, after Hannah had conceived, that she gave birth to a son; and she named him Samuel, saying, "Because I have asked him of the Lord."

Then the man Elkanah went up with all his household to offer to the Lord the yearly sacrifice and pay his vow. But Hannah did not go up, for she said to her husband, "I will not go up until the child is weaned; then I will bring him, that he may appear before the Lord and stay there forever." And Elkanah her husband said to her, "Do what seems best to you. Remain until you have weaned him; only may the Lord confirm His word." So the woman remained and nursed her son until she weaned him.

Now when she had weaned him, she took him up with her, with a three-year-old bull and one ephah of flour and a jug of wine, and brought him to the house of the Lord in Shiloh, although the child was young. Then they slaughtered the bull, and brought the boy to Eli. And she said, "Oh, my lord! As your soul lives, my lord, I am the woman who stood here beside you, praying to the Lord. For this boy I prayed, and the Lord has given me my petition which I asked of Him. So I have also dedicated him to the Lord; as long as he lives he is dedicated to the Lord." And he worshipped the Lord there.

Were the difficulties in her marriage partly her fault? Had she like Sarah prompted her husband to take a concubine when he discovered that they wouldn't have children?[1] Or had she been unable to resist Elkanah's love, becoming his second wife after he had married Peninnah already?

In either case Hannah certainly had not foreseen the far-reaching consequences of her actions. The second marriage had resulted in terrible misery for each of the three marriage partners.

Maybe Hannah was not at fault. Had Elkanah, an otherwise God-fearing man, become a bigamist on his own initiative? Whatever the cause, her experiences were nonetheless painful.

The Holy Spirit did not think it was necessary to register these details. But the Bible does say that Hannah was a woman who had

---

1. Genesis 16:1,2

definite access to God. The way to Him was open to her on the basis of forgiveness of sin by means of the sacrifices that her husband, as head of the family, regularly made to the Lord.

Sometimes a person is tested to his very roots of being, and it seems as if some unseen power is operating to extinguish his life. Hannah must have felt that way. She had shed countless tears because she felt forsaken by God since she had no children. Her husband's other wife never let an opportunity pass by without reminding her of her childlessness.

Elkanah, wanting to comfort Hannah, had told her that he loved her the most. Wasn't his love more to her than ten sons? She had been happy with this expression of his love, but these words had also given her food for thought and made her even more lonesome. Had Elkanah given up the hope of ever having a child by her?

Abraham, she remembered, had wrestled with God about a child.[2] Isaac, in a similar situation, had prayed for his wife.[3] And their wives had given birth, even late in life, to sons who had come to mean so much to her people. Those sons had been part of God's plan for Israel.

God! He is the only One who understands me, the only One who can help me, she thought. She went back to the tabernacle, alone. There she broke down before God. Heartbroken, without words. At first she wasn't even able to voice her thoughts.

Then, when her heart had somewhat unburdened itself, her lips breathed a prayer, though her voice remained silent. "O Lord of hosts . . . " she began. The way she spoke to Him declared her vision of Him. He was the Lord of the hosts of heaven and earth, of everything He had created.[4] An immense host of angels stood at His disposal.[5] He was the Lord who had performed many miracles for Israel as a nation.

Those four words, "O Lord of hosts," expressed her faith in His greatness and might. (Commentator Matthew Henry says this was the first time a person had addressed God in this manner.) *In light of His majesty I am nothing,* she thought. *Only a servant, a handmaid.* She repeated this thought three times. The words were chosen carefully. She considered herself an insignificant earthly

2. Genesis 15:2-6
3. Genesis 25:21
4. Genesis 2:1
5. Genesis 32:1,2; Luke 2:13

creature in the light of a holy God, yet she wanted to serve Him. This was a proper set of values, for she—though a lowly human being—could serve God.

Realizing this, Hannah presented God with a great petition. She did not insult Him by asking for a small favor. One doesn't ask for a few pennies from a multimillionaire. From such a great God one shouldn't expect anything short of a miracle—a real miracle.

Hannah didn't pray vaguely. She made a specific request, "God, I want to have a son." Her prayer was followed by a promise, "Then I will give him back to You for all of his life, and no razor will ever touch his head." Her son, if God granted him, would be a Nazarite, a man dedicated to Him, who would drink no wine and who would never cut his hair.[6]

Was Hannah actually saying, "God, You know that I desire to have a child, but even more than asking this for myself, I ask this for You"? It is possible.

The religion of her people, that is, the religion of its priests had lost its meaning. It had been corrupted. Yet Hannah had preserved her faith, and kept it pure. However, her influence was limited. What the country needed was a man who could become a link between God and His people, who could breach the gap and usher in a new future.

Did Hannah's heart cry out only for herself, or was she also weeping for God and for her people? Was this why her prayer had such a far-reaching impact? Did she realize what part she could have in the spiritual solution of this national problem? It is possible, though the scriptural record is too brief to determine this.

The decay of the people and the priesthood was also indicated by Eli's treatment of her. He had little human understanding, little compassion.

"How long will you be drunk?" he lashed out at her. "Put away your wine." The priest who hadn't dared deal harshly with his own sons felt no reservation in dealing with Hannah. The old man revealed a lack of insight and poor self-control.

His words also revealed that in those days drunk people and bad women were not an unusual sight in the house of God. Even Eli's own sons slept with the women who gathered at the door of the tabernacle.[7]

6. Judges 13:3-5; Luke 1:15; Amos 2:12

Hannah, however, was in the presence of God and so felt no desire to defend or justify herself. She didn't express any shame or indignation, but explained the situation in a few words. Eli suddenly became what he should have been—the priest of God. As the representative of the Lord, he said, "Go in peace. The God of Israel will grant your petition." He didn't know the nature of her request, but as instructed by God, he told her she had been heard.

With these words the peace of God which follows each faithful prayer came into her heart.[8] She had taken her cares to God and left them in His hands.

"Now faith is the assurance of things hoped for, the conviction of things not seen," the author of the Epistle to the Hebrews wrote many centuries later.[9] That was what Hannah experienced. The assurance that her prayer was heard entered her heart. Outwardly the change was remarkable—her appetite returned and her face no longer held any trace of sadness. She lived her faith, trusting God in such a way that other people noticed it.

Samuel, which means "heard of God," was born a year later. Then the meaning of her own name—"gracious" or "favor"— began to make sense. Instead of being a neglected woman, she had become an extraordinarily privileged one, for her prayer marked a turning point in history.

It was not long before God's Word was again heard in all of Israel.[10] The Lord revealed Himself through Samuel even when Samuel was still a boy. From Dan, far to the north, to Beersheba, far to the south, the people acknowledged that Samuel was a prophet appointed by God.[11]

The people turned from idols to serve God. The ark of the Lord, which had been taken for spoil and dishonored by the Philistines, was returned.[12] The Philistines made peace with Israel, for the hand of the Lord was against the Philistines all the days of Samuel. Cities were regained which had been lost in battle.

The faith of Hannah lived in her son. Centuries later his name would be listed among the heroes of faith,[13] for he was one of the men who through faith had subdued kingdoms.

Samuel, who had been born in answer to prayer and whose name constantly reminded him of that, became a man of prayer himself. He felt it was sin for people not to pray.[14] This attitude

---

7. I Samuel 2:22
8. Philippians 4:6,7
9. Hebrews 11:1

10. I Samuel 4:1
11. I Samuel 3:19-21
12. I Samuel 6 and 7

13. Hebrews 11:32,33

may have been the key to the many answers he received.

Only eternity will reveal what Israel, whom he served as a prophet, priest and judge, and the millions who have since studied his life, owe to Samuel's life and ministry.

Oh, Hannah, were you not favored when you saw the results of the answer to your prayer? And were you not as privileged as Sarah and Rebekah to see your child playing such a role in history?

Mary, the mother of Christ, must have been influenced by Hannah's prayer and her touching song of praise when she offered her Magnificat.[15] Hannah had a wonderful time during the period in which her child grew from a baby to a toddler. It passed quickly, however. And, as soon as Samuel was weaned, she fulfilled her promise and gave him back to God from whom she had received him. From then on, she saw him only once a year, when she and her husband offered their sacrifices in Shiloh.[16]

Her prayer was radical in nature. So was her dedication. She had to offer Samuel to God daily, trusting Him to protect Samuel's faith in the midst of the corruption he saw in Eli and his sons.

Prayer, faith and dedication continued to characterize her life, for Hannah knew that a person who gave all to God would receive more in return. God will never be any person's debtor. He gave her five more children.

Why could Hannah count on answered prayer? Because she had met God's prerequisites. These prerequisites were not neatly collected in a single passage of Scripture, but they were principles which, in her walk with God, she sensed and knew. These included:

1. Praying because of sin forgiven.[17]
2. Pleading in God's name, acknowledging His greatness.[18]
3. Being impressed by one's own nothingness.[19]
4. Formulating a clear, well-defined petition.[20]
5. Desiring that God's will be done and His Kingdom extended.[21]
6. Praying in faith.[22]

---

14. I Samuel 12:23

15. Luke 1:46-55

16. I Samuel 2:19-21

17. Psalm 66:13-19

18. John 16:24

19. II Samuel 7:18-29

20. Matthew 7:7-11

21. I John 5:14,15

22. Hebrews 11:6; Matthew 21:22

Hannah, a woman who believed in prayer
(I Samuel 1:9-28. Also see verses under Peninnah.)

Questions:
1. Read Judges 21:25 and I Samuel 2:11-36. What was the situation of her people, nationally and spiritually?
2. Compare Hannah's prayer carefully with the Lord's prayer (Matthew 6:9-13). What resemblances do you see?
3. On what basis can you conclude that Hannah counted on answered prayer?
4. What struck you most in connection with Hannah's dedication to God?
5. Hannah's song of praise (I Samuel 2:1-10) reveals her deepest thoughts. What does she think of God?
6. What did Hannah receive in return for the son she dedicated to God? (I Samuel 2:21) What does that prove?
7. What changes do you see in Israel, nationally and spiritually, after Samuel's arrival? (I Samuel 3:19 to 4:1; chapters 6 and 7)
8. In what ways can Hannah's example influence your prayer life?

9

"Since the day before yesterday I have been called to a task so heavy that no one who even for a moment considers the weight thereof should desire it, but also so wonderful that all I can say is, who am I that I am privileged to do this."
Queen Juliana of the Netherlands*

The Queen of Sheba, a woman who desired to be wiser

I Kings 10:1-10,13 Now when the Queen of Sheba heard about the fame of Solomon concerning the name of the Lord, she came to test him with difficult questions. So she came to Jerusalem with a very large retinue, with camels carrying spices and very much gold and precious stones. When she came to Solomon, she spoke with him about all that was in her heart. And Solomon answered all her questions; nothing was hidden from the king which he did not explain to her. When the Queen of Sheba perceived all the wisdom of Solomon, the house that he had built, the food of his table, the seating of his servants, the attendance of his waiters and their attire, his cupbearers, and his stairway by which he went up to the house of the Lord, there was no more spirit in her. Then she said to the king, "It was a true report which I heard in my own land about your words and your wisdom. Nevertheless I did not believe the reports, until I came and my eyes had seen it. And behold, the half was not told me. You exceed in wisdom and prosperity the report which I heard. How blessed are your men, how blessed are these your servants who stand before you continually and hear your wisdom. Blessed be the Lord your God who delighted in you to set you on the throne of Israel; because the Lord loved Israel forever, therefore He made you king, to do justice and righteousness." And

*In her address when ascending the throne, September 6, 1948.

she gave the king a hundred and twenty talents of gold, and a very great amount of spices and precious stones. Never again did such abundance of spices come in as that which the Queen of Sheba gave King Solomon . . . . And King Solomon gave to the Queen of Sheba all her desire which she requested, besides what he gave her according to his royal bounty. Then she turned and went to her own land together with her servants.

Matthew 12:42 The Queen of the South shall rise up with this generation at the judgment and shall condemn it, because she came from the ends of the earth to hear the wisdom of Solomon; and behold, something greater than Solomon is here.

Slowly, the long caravan crept along the ascending road from Jericho to Jerusalem. The heavily loaded camels carried their burdens with nodding heads. The men tending them drove them onward, knowing that the end of the long trip was in sight.

The woman in the center of the party who had arranged the trip wondered if the exertion of the strenuous journey would be rewarded. It had taken weeks to cover more than two thousand miles. The cold nights and scorchingly hot days had seemed endless. The countryside had been as sunbaked and unpleasant as a moonscape. Worst of all were the lashing sandstorms and raging winds of the wilderness.

But in her heart she knew she must go. At home in her royal palace in Sheba, she had heard repeatedly about Solomon, the king of Israel, the man who appeared to be immensely rich and unbelievably wise. His fame was known throughout the East. The whole earth consulted Solomon, to hear the wisdom God had put in his heart.[1] Many kings visited and consulted with him. They honored him with rich gifts.[2]

She had many questions—about her personal life, about her royal obligations, about God.

The remarkable thing about the rumors she had heard about Solomon was that they were always connected with the name of the Lord. Yahweh, the God of Israel, was said to be the source of his prosperity. She knew many gods herself—gods of the sea, and of the land, of war, of wine, of day and of night, but they had never

---

1. I Kings 10:24
2. II Chronicles 9:22-24

given a solution to any problem. Would this One be able to do that?

The way the queen ordered her priorities proves she was a wise woman. In her wisdom, she accepted the limitations of her own knowledge and insight. She wanted to know more and was willing to make many sacrifices in order to gain wisdom. Her time, money and effort were spent in attaining this goal.

True wisdom goes hand in hand with humility. The Queen of Sheba was humble enough to tell the outside world that she was searching for more and that she was not satisfied with her state. Anyone who saw the passing caravan knew that the Queen of Sheba was enroute to Jerusalem to consult the wise Solomon.

As she came around the last bend in the road, she saw the city of Jerusalem situated on the mountains. Some of the dominant buildings drew her attention, particularly the palace of the king and the Temple of his God. Behind her trudged the camels, bent under their costly burdens of rare spices, gold and precious stones, the value of which could not even be guessed. (One estimate of a hundred and twenty talents of gold would be worth about 26 million dollars today.)

Solomon, the tenth son of David and the second of his union with Bathsheba, was the third king of Israel. He was also called by the prophet Nathan and according to God's will, Jedidiah, which means, "loved by God."[3]

After he had inherited the throne from his father, God had appeared to him in a dream one night and asked him, "What shall I give you?" The reply of the young man showed his humility and dependence, "Give Your servant an understanding mind to govern, so that I may discern good from evil; for who is able to govern Your great people?"[4] The answer was so well pleasing in the sight of God that He added riches and honor to a wisdom so great that it would never be equaled. Solomon rose head and shoulders above all other kings. His people experienced a golden era in their history.

At this time in history Egypt, Assyria and Babylon were weak. The great days of Homer's Greece were yet ahead. Israel was the mightiest kingdom in the world. Jerusalem was the most beautiful

3. II Samuel 12:24,25
4. I Kings 3:5-14

city. No building could compare in beauty with the Temple. In this setting, one monarch went to visit another. It was not a state visit, but one of a private nature.

The conversation was stimulating. The queen was humble enough to reveal her hunger for wisdom. She asked Solomon many questions. Solomon, she found, was an open man—a person with seemingly infinite understanding. Like her, he also filled the high, but lonely role of a ruler. Consequently, he was someone who could understand her fully. He himself had wrestled with the same problems.

To her amazement and admiration there was no question too deep or too involved for him. He had an answer for everything. She saw that he truly was blessed by God. He had not only intellectual wisdom, but common sense knowledge which was applicable in practical, daily situations. She saw this in the way his house had been built, in the manners of his servants and ministers, in the quality of his meals and in the variety of the drinks. Every detail of his life was permeated with wisdom. Also, his faith in God affected every aspect of his life. It was pure. It was real. It was the center of his existence.

King Solomon not only involved her in his daily duties, he also shared how he served God with her. And there she discovered the true secret of his successful life. When Solomon offered his burnt offerings to God, he identified himself with the innocent animal that was being slaughtered in his place, for his sin.[5] This revealed a seed of truth to the Queen of Sheba.

Solomon's life was freed because his sins were forgiven; this fact was based on God's appointed means. The shed blood of an innocent creature guaranteed that he—the guilty one—could exist in full freedom.[6] His fellowship with God was the source of all his wisdom, his understanding[7] and his prosperity.[8]

Solomon's aim in life, she discovered, was not to learn and teach wisdom, but to fear God. Solomon kept His commandments and declared emphatically that this was what God desired of all men, including kings.[9]

The queen was amazed. She was without words. Her highest expectations had been exceeded. "I didn't believe what I heard

5. Leviticus 1:1-9; 9:7
6. Leviticus 17:11   8. Proverbs 10:22
7. Proverbs 2:6; 9:10   9. Ecclesiastes 12:9-13

about your wisdom," she said. "It seemed too omnipotent. But the truth greatly surpassed all rumors. I hadn't heard half of it."

The queen envied the people who served this king, the subjects over whom he had authority. She acknowledged that wisdom was to be preferred above all else.[10] Most remarkably, she stated that Solomon was a love gift from God to His people, so that they might be ruled well.

She had been enriched mentally and materially by her meeting with King Solomon. The king shared graciously with her not only his vast understanding, but riches that excelled the precious gifts she had brought him.[11] The worth of the most valued gift she received could not be given a monetary figure. For it was the knowledge she gained about God, who is the source of true wisdom.[12]

The Queen of Sheba was a woman who made history. Even Jesus Christ cited her as an example. He praised her for sparing no cost or trouble to hear the wisdom of Solomon. By that action she condemned those who don't take wisdom seriously. She provides a splendid example of the importance of subjecting the things of God to a closer investigation. And she provided proof of her deep insight when she accepted the opportunity to learn from someone else—someone who was wiser than she.[13] She didn't just listen to the rumors that Solomon was a wise man. She did everything possible to seek him out to discover the source of his wisdom.[14]

But was her only enrichment intellectual? Was that her sole satisfaction? Or did her heart stretch out to God Himself, the Source of wisdom,[15] the God with whom even Solomon could not be compared? For the greatest wisdom comes not from the mind, but from the heart. The expectation of such a man shall not be cut off.[16]

James, the practical apostle, wrote a thousand years later that a man fools himself when he listens to a message but does not put it into practice. He is like a person who sees his face in a mirror, sees that his appearance needs correction and then fails to do anything about it (James 1:22-24).

Was the queen truly wise? Did she fully understand all Solomon told her? Did she apply the wisdom she saw in Solomon? Was her heart changed? Did she fulfill the objectives of the plan she had set out to accomplish?[17] Completely?

Her search was a failure if she did not find God. Then she would

---

10. Proverbs 8:11   13. Ephesians 5:16

11. II Chronicles 9:12   14. Proverbs 2:1-6   16. Proverbs 24:14

12. Ecclesiastes 2:26   15. Isaiah 11:2; I Corinthians 1:30   17. II Corinthians 8:10,11

be a tragic figure, instead of the perfect example she is. The Bible does not answer these questions directly. But perhaps the answer can be found in Jesus' words when He put her above the Jews, using her as an example to some Pharisees and scribes of His time. Isn't this proof that she learned her lessons? The Queen of Sheba was a woman who spared no cost or trouble to become wiser.

The Queen of Sheba, a woman who desired to be wiser
(I Kings 10:1-10,13; Matthew 12:42)

Questions:
1. What was the fame of Solomon, which the Queen of Sheba heard about, connected with?
2. In what ways did she show her sincere interest to profit from his wisdom?
3. What further shows her openness to learn? What conclusions did she come to after she had seen everything with her own eyes?
4. What do you consider to be the most remarkable conclusion of this heathen queen?
5. The Lord Jesus praises her for the seriousness with which she sought the wisdom of Solomon. Do you have any reason to conclude that her visit led her into a personal relationship with God?
6. Do you consider her to be a good example or a warning for you? What can you do with what you have learned from her?

10

*"Faith is not merely an act, but a series of acts.
It is a maintained attitude of the heart, an unquestioned
obedience. Faith must have a divine warrant upon
which to rest, and it finds this in the promises of God."*

J. Oswald Sanders*

The widow of Zarephath,
a woman who accepted the challenge of faith

I Kings 17:7-24 And it happened after a while, that the brook dried up, because there was no rain in the land.

Then the word of the Lord came to him, saying, "Arise, go to Zarephath, which belongs to Sidon, and stay there; behold, I have commanded a widow there to provide for you." So he arose and went to Zarephath, and when he came to the gate of the city, behold, a widow was there gathering sticks; and he called to her and said, "Please get me a little water in a jar, that I may drink." And as she was going to get it, he called to her and said, "Please bring me a piece of bread in your hand." But she said, "As the Lord your God lives, I have no bread, only a handful of flour in the bowl and a little oil in the jar; and behold, I am gathering a few sticks that I may go in and prepare for me and my son, that we may eat it and die." Then Elijah said to her, "Do not fear; go, do as you have said, but make me a little bread cake from it first, and bring it out to me, and afterward you may make one for yourself and for your son. For thus says the Lord God of Israel, 'The bowl of flour shall not be exhausted, nor shall the jar of oil be empty, until the day that the Lord sends rain on the face of the earth.'" So she went and did according to the word of Elijah, and she and he and her household ate for many days. The bowl of flour was not exhausted nor did the

*Sanders, J. Oswald. *Mighty Faith,*
© 1971, Moody Press, Chicago, Illinois.

jar of oil become empty, according to the word of the Lord which He spoke through Elijah.

Now it came about after these things, that the son of the woman, the mistress of the house, became sick; and his sickness was so severe, that there was no breath left in him. So she said to Elijah, "What do I have to do with you, O man of God? You have come to me to bring my iniquity to remembrance, and to put my son to death!" And he said to her, "Give me your son." Then he took him from her bosom and carried him up to the upper room where he was living, and laid him on his own bed. And he called to the Lord and said, "O Lord my God, hast Thou also brought calamity to the widow with whom I am staying, by causing her son to die?" Then he stretched himself upon the child three times, and called to the Lord, and said, "O Lord my God, I pray Thee, let this child's life return to him." And the Lord heard the voice of Elijah, and the life of the child returned to him and he revived. And Elijah took the child, and brought him down from the upper room into the house and gave him to his mother; and Elijah said, "See, your son is alive." Then the woman said to Elijah, "Now I know that you are a man of God, and that the word of the Lord in your mouth is truth."

She lived in the little harbor town of Zarephath between Tyre and Sidon in Phoenicia. Her husband was dead. She and her little son were near death as well, for there was a terrible drought in the land. There had been no rain for many days. The water supplies had been exhausted and the land was incapable of producing any crops. Food supplies were running out and could not be replenished. The difficulties of daily living were mounting not only for this widow but for every other inhabitant of the country.

She had a little oil and flour left—just enough to prepare a final meal for herself and her child. After eating this, they could only wait for death. She went out to gather wood to prepare their last meal. When she arrived at the city gate she saw a man in a long, loose garment held together with a leather belt. She did not know him for he was a stranger. He was Elijah, a prophet of Israel.

He called to her and asked her to bring a little water in a vessel for him to drink.

She realized that he was a holy man. She could see that by his clothes. Though she had no water to spare she felt she could not disappoint him. She must do what he requested. The God of Elijah was not her god. She was a heathen. But she had heard enough about the God of Israel to feel a deep respect and awe for Him. As she turned to go back home for the water, he said, "Bring me a morsel of bread in your hand."

She explained the situation to him saying, "As the Lord your God lives, I don't have anything baked. All I have is a handful of meal and a little oil in a cruse. I am out gathering some sticks in order to prepare this for my son and myself so we may eat it, and die." She expected her somber story would convince him that, unfortunately, she could not comply with his request. But this was not the case for he replied, "Don't be afraid. Go and fix the meal as you have planned, but first make me a little cake and bring it to me. Then afterward make some for yourself and your son. For the Lord, the God of Israel, promises that the jar of meal will not run out and the cruse of oil will not fail until the Lord again sends rain upon the earth."

She had never before had anything which couldn't run out. Personally she had never had any dealings with the God of Israel. Although this man spoke in the name of God, what guarantee did she have that he was sent by Him? She was willing to take the risk for herself, but she had to consider the life of her child. Her only child—

A great act of faith was being asked of this heathen woman. She was challenged to believe the word of a man when she didn't have any proof that he was even a servant of God. How could she trust him?

But she sensed an authority in the voice of the man. She decided to take the risk. And after she had served the prophet his meal, there was still flour and oil left over for her and her son!

This miracle repeated itself for many days. The experience was similar to God's continued provision of bread to the Israelites in the wilderness.[1] It continued to be a daily challenge of her faith. The supply was always of such scanty measure that she could not put any food aside and trust in it. She could

Faith cannot be separated from the object in which it believes. Without the reliability of the object, faith can become an unbridled emotion or a presumption without any promise to sustain it. Faith cannot be disconnected from the Word of God.

1. Exodus 16

only trust in the promise of God.

So every day an act of faith was required from her, faith in the word that was spoken. And daily she, her son and Elijah experienced a miracle, for every day there was enough for all of them to eat. This continued for many days. Her faith became anchored in God.

Then something occurred which was impossible for her to understand. Elijah had come to live in her home, using the spare upper room. The author of Hebrews states that a person who is hospitable may lodge angels unaware.[2] This was her experience. The angel of death, busily at work during a time of famine, did not enter her door, and she did not fall victim to him.

Therefore, it was inconceivable to her that her son should suddenly become ill. Even before she had time to tell the prophet, her son died. She didn't understand! Why had God kept the child alive during the famine only to allow him to die? Death was snatching his prey from an entirely different angle. This puzzled her.

With the presence of the holy man of God in her house, she had come to realize that she was a sinful woman. Was this why her son had died? Did sin demand a penalty? She confronted the prophet with this question. She was desperate.

"Give me your son," Elijah said. He took the dead boy up to his room and put him on his own bed. Then he wrestled with God in prayer about the child. "O Lord my God, have You brought calamity to the widow with whom I board by slaying her son? Return this child's soul to him again," he begged, while stretching himself upon the child three times. It seemed as if he wanted to transmit his life and the warmth of his body into the cold, still form of the boy. To his unspeakable joy, God answered his prayer. He saw life flowing back into the child. He returned the boy alive to his mother.

Meanwhile, the widow experienced a crisis in her faith. The miracle of the multiplication of the food had strengthened her faith in the prophet's mandate. His commission was true. He did speak the Word of God. He could be trusted. She had never expressed this clearly in words. She was so closely connected with the present drama, so captured by surprise and so shocked, that she was

---

unable to realize that God was doing something wonderful for her.

Deep suffering should stimulate greater faith. Such a faith, however, must first be tested for genuineness. God wants to know its value and, therefore, allows suffering. The faith that remains after the test of suffering is pure.[3]

Later, when the famine was over she would look back and experience a double blessing for she had not only experienced having her life prolonged day by day, but she had also experienced a resurrection from the dead. The resurrection of her small son is the first biblical record of a person being raised from death.

As a result of this experience, she made a clear statement of faith, "Now I know that you are a man of God, and that the words that you speak are true." She would never again doubt the Word of God. The second test of faith was much more difficult than the first, but she came through, matured and enriched.

These miracles didn't happen in Israel. Could no one be found among God's own people, among those who had rejected Him to serve Baal, to help His threatened prophet? Was God forced to look for help outside Israel's borders? In this difficult period in the history of His people, God kept His servant alive by means of a heathen woman, a widow who accepted the challenge to have faith in the Word of God.

This woman learned that God puts a high reward on faith.[4] She developed a sensitivity for the unseen, yet very real world of faith. The testing that God put her through enabled her to understand the reality, assurance and proof of His faithfulness.[5]

The widow of Zarephath, a woman who accepted the challenge of faith
(I Kings 17:7-24)

Questions:
1. What was the situation of the widow of Zarephath and her son when Elijah met her?

---

3. I Peter 1:6,7; 4:12,13
4. Hebrews 11:6   5. Hebrews 11:1,2

2. Describe the extent of Elijah's request. What enormous challenge of faith did he offer her with his request?
3. What was her reaction? What did she prove by her reaction?
4. For a long time the family depended upon God's miracle of multiplication. What do you consider to be the most outstanding experience for the widow in that situation? (Compare with Exodus 16 and Matthew 6:25-34.)
5. I Peter 1:6,7 requests that faith be tried for its genuineness. Read I Kings 17:17-24 again, especially the last verse. How did the widow experience this and how did she stand the trial?
6. Does the good example of this woman offer a challenge to you? Do you see ways you can practice your faith better? If so, how will you do it?

11

*"Elisha—did he ever look through his windows down
the next 28 centuries, and contemplate what multiplicities
of comfort to 'prophets' yet unborn would during that
time develop from his aboriginal bed, table, stool
and candlestick?"* Theron Brown*

The Shunammite,
a creative thinker

II Kings 4:8-22, 32-37 Now there came a day when Elisha passed
over to Shunem, where there was a prominent woman, and she
persuaded him to eat food. And so it was, as often as he passed by,
he turned in there to eat food. And she said to her husband, "Behold
now, I perceive that this is a holy man of God passing by us
continually. Please, let us make a little walled upper chamber and
let us set a bed for him there, and a table and a chair and a
lampstand; and it shall be, when he comes to us, that he can turn in
there." One day he came there and turned in to the upper chamber
and rested. Then he said to Gehazi his servant, "Call this
Shunammite." And when he had called her, she stood before him.
And he said to him, "Say now to her, 'Behold, you have been careful
for us with all this care; what can I do for you? Would you be spoken
for to the king or to the captain of the army?'" And she answered, "I
live among my own people." So he said, "What then is to be done for
her?" And Gehazi answered, "Truly she has no son and her
husband is old." And he said, "Call her." When he had called her,
she stood in the doorway. Then he said, "At this season next year
you shall embrace a son." And she said, "No, my lord, O man of
God, do not lie to your maidservant." And the woman conceived

*Lockyer, Herbert, R.S.L. *The Women of the Bible,*
© 1967, Zondervan Publishing House, Grand Rapids, Michigan.

and bore a son at that season the next year, as Elisha had said to her.

When the child was grown, the day came that he went out to his father to the reapers. And he said to his father, "My head, my head." And he said to his servant, "Carry him to his mother." When he had taken him and brought him to his mother, he sat on her lap until noon, and then died. And she went up and laid him on the bed of the man of God, and shut the door behind him, and went out. Then she called to her husband and said, "Please send me one of the servants and one of the donkeys, that I may run to the man of God and return. . . . "

When Elisha came into the house, behold the lad was dead and laid on his bed. So he entered and shut the door behind them both, and prayed to the Lord. And he went up and lay on the child, and put his mouth on his mouth and his eyes on his eyes and his hands on his hands, and he stretched himself on him; and the flesh of the child became warm. Then he returned and walked in the house once back and forth, and went up and stretched himself on him; and the lad sneezed seven times and the lad opened his eyes. And he called Gehazi and said, "Call this Shunammite." So he called her. And when she came in to him, he said, "Take up your son." Then she went in and fell at his feet and bowed herself to the ground, and she took up her son and went out.

With a few strong lines, the Bible draws her portrait—a great woman, very rich, married to an older man, childless. Her name is not mentioned. She was called the Shunammite after the name of her city.

Shunem was situated a little north of Jezreel near Nain, a city which became well known nearly 900 years later because Jesus raised a widow's son from death there.

The Bible leaves no doubt that the husband was the head of the family. This did not mean, however, that the woman was a drudge who could only give her assent—a person who displayed no personal initiative. The Shunammite woman was the most energetic, since she was the younger of the pair. She offered ideas, but only carried them out after discussing them with her husband. She shared her plans with him, and decisionmaking was a joint effort.

Mature characters don't desire to dominate. Instead, they seek to work harmoniously with one another so that the marriage can function according to God's will. This can take place even when other factors, such as a great difference in age, are not particularly favorable. God creates each human being uniquely. It is up to each individual—husband or wife—to realize what his or her gifts are and to use them to their full potential.

The Shunammite woman was extremely rich and could easily have allowed herself to become undisciplined, enjoying all the things money could buy. Being a childless woman with an old husband, she could have easily led a dried-up life without purpose, nursing self-pity. But she didn't.

This woman had a wealth of interest in the world around her. She thought of others first, not of herself. She watched her environment attentively and had noticed among the many who passed her house daily that one individual was exceptional. Being hospitable, she invited him to a meal, for she realized that he was, indeed, an unusual person. He was the prophet Elisha.

While she, as a housewife, took care of her daily responsibilities, she asked herself the question, *What can I do for this servant of God?* She received what was, certainly for her time, an original idea—*I'll make a guest room for him! Not a temporal, tent-like thing, but something which is solid and will last.* With her husband's help, she built a guest room for Elisha on the upper level of the house.

The Shunammite, in desiring to serve God, received a creative idea from Him. She created something new, something usable for His service.

There was a bed, table, stool and lampstand in the room. She made it a room where Elisha could work as well as sleep. She didn't forget anything.

So Elisha stayed with them. Everything had been arranged for prolonged and repeated usage. Undoubtedly, there was also room for his servant Gehazi. She enjoyed using her money to support the Lord's prophet. Instead of offering money so Elisha could secure lodging and food for himself, she took the trouble to build brand new quarters for him. In sharing her possessions, she gave of herself. As a result, God rewarded her.

Elisha had asked her through his servant Gehazi, "Since you have taken all this trouble for us, what can we do for you?"

The grateful woman had replied that she had no request for she had everything she needed. The observant Gehazi later pointed out to his master, "She has no son, and her husband is old."

But, when she had received the promise that she would bear a son, she didn't dare believe it. "No, my lord, O man of God; please do not lie to your maidservant." But it had not been a deception. It was real. A godly reality! A year later she gave birth to a son.

One day when the little boy was about three or four years old, he accompanied his father to the fields. There he became ill and died within a few hours. His mother put his dead body on the bed of the prophet in the room where he prayed and meditated. She saw only one possible solution—God!

Since God had given her this son, He was the only One who could help. She rushed to His representative, Elisha, who was then at Carmel. Had her thoughts wandered back to that other prophet, Elijah, who had also raised a child from the dead, the child of the widow of Zarephath? Didn't his spirit rest upon Elisha?

There was no time to waste. Though she informed her husband she was going to visit the prophet, she didn't waste time with further explanations. Had a distance of 25 miles ever seemed so long before? *Is it sensible of me to make this trip,* she asked herself, *since my son is dead already?*

Elisha could see from a distance that something was wrong. He wanted to send his servant Gehazi back with her to help. But she was not satisfied with that. She told Elisha she would return only if he himself would go with her. Before having her son she had been satisfied with her situation in life. She hadn't asked Elisha for a son, but now she missed her child dearly. She felt that the only one who could help her was the man who was instrumental in helping her get the child from God. Since she had totally dedicated herself to meeting Elisha's needs, she now expected him to return with her. Elisha was persuaded and went with her.

When they arrived at her home, Elisha, just as Elijah had before him, stretched himself over the tiny corpse and raised him from death. The Shunammite then received her son for the second time. First she had received him at birth, now she received him from the dead. She did not need to make funeral preparations, so she prepared for a feast!

This was not the only blessing bestowed upon the Shunammite. When the country was threatened by a famine some years later, she was warned by the prophet in time to move away with her family and escape starvation. Not until seven years later did she return to her country. During her absence she had lost her home and fields. She asked the king to restore these to her. He not only did that, he also gave her all of its fruits![1]

Why? Because she was the woman whose son Elisha had restored to life and because of her contribution to him and the Kingdom of God.

The Shunammite was just a woman. But she was a woman who thought creatively. A woman who, by her unselfish dedication to someone else, opened the floodgates of blessing upon herself. The person who gives becomes the one who receives. This is always true for a person who trusts in God.[2]

The story of the Shunammite woman is similar to the story of the home in Bethany where Jesus and His disciples were lodged often and gladly. There too a person was raised from the dead: Lazarus (Luke 10:38-42; John 11:1-44; 12:1).

Creativity comes from the Latin word *creatus* and is related to the word "creator." It was the Shunammite woman's relationship with God, the Creator, that made her what she was.

A genuine walk with God leads to creativity. The person who asks how he can serve God with what he has receives ideas, so to speak, straight from heaven. These are not emotional or presumptuous ideas, but practical and usable ones within the framework of the potential God gives to each person. God's Holy Spirit inspires creativity.

For the Shunammite this did not mean laboring directly for the temple of God, like Bezalel and Oholiab, the designers of the tabernacle.[3] Instead, she served God within her own home. By doing so she scratched away the label of "routine" from the occupation of "housewife." She used her material possessions for the well-being of others. A study of her life reveals that God rewards this.

1. II Kings 8:1-6
2. Luke 6:38   3. Exodus 31:1-11

The Shunammite, a creative thinker
(II Kings 4:8-22, 32-37)

Questions:

1. Describe the situation and the character of the Shunammite.
2. Why did she gladly offer hospitality to Elisha?
3. What new ideas did she utilize to help the prophet? What does this prove?
4. What lessons do you observe in this story in regard to hospitality? (See also Luke 6:38.)
5. What parallel do you see with another hospitable home in the Bible? (Luke 10:38- 42; John 11:1- 44; 12:1,2)
6. The Shunammite developed creative ideas for the service of the Kingdom of God. Are there ways in which you could follow her example? Describe how.

12

*"The question for each man to settle is not what
he would do for the Lord if he had more money, time
or education, but what he will do with the things he has.
It's not who you are or what you have that matters—
but whether Christ controls you."*
Author unknown

A Jewish maid,
the girl who talked about God

II Kings 5:1-5,14,15 Now Naaman, captain of the army of the king of
Syria, was a great man with his master, and highly respected,
because by him the Lord had given victory to Syria. The man was
also a valiant warrior, but he was a leper. Now the Syrians had gone
out in bands, and had taken captive a little girl from the land of
Israel; and she waited on Naaman's wife. And she said to her
mistress, "I wish that my master were with the prophet who is in
Samaria! Then he would cure him of his leprosy." And Naaman
went in and told his master, saying, "Thus and thus spoke the girl
who is from the land of Israel." Then the king of Syria said, "Go
now, and I will send a letter to the king of Israel." And he departed
and took with him ten talents of silver and six thousand shekels of
gold and ten changes of clothes. . . .

So he went down and dipped himself seven times in the Jordan,
according to the word of the man of God; and his flesh was restored
like the flesh of a little child, and he was clean.

When he returned to the man of God with all his company, and
came and stood before him, he said, "Behold now, I know that there
is no God in all the earth, but in Israel; so please take a present from
your servant now."

Acts 1:8 But you shall receive power when the Holy Spirit has come upon you; and you shall be My witnesses both in Jerusalem, and in all Judea and Samaria, and even to the remotest part of the earth."

850 B.C. Officially there was peace in Israel. However, the troops of Syria's King Ben-hadad kept making raids into Israel to capture prisoners as spoil. One day they captured a young Jewish girl who was not more than 15 years old. Her name is not recorded in the Bible. Perhaps this is because what is told about her is so impressive that her name is of secondary importance.

The girl became the maid of the wife of a high ranking officer in the king's army. The officer, Naaman, was capable and very influential. He was greatly honored by the king because of his valor in combat. Was it a result of the prayers of her God-fearing parents or was it the answer to her own heart-cry to God that the little maid arrived, probably via the slave market in Damascus, in this good home?

At the moment Naaman was deeply worried. A shadow had fallen over his house that couldn't be driven away. He had realized that he had leprosy, the most dreadful of diseases. Once a person contracted leprosy, he was outcast for the rest of his life.[1] It was a horrible disease, and it might take years before death freed the sufferer from his isolation.

Naaman was a dead man already. His physical death might be many years in the future, but in reality, for his wife, his master, his colleagues and for the little maid, he would soon no longer exist. No king, no trophy of victory could prevent his expulsion. He would be forced to wander outside the city walls as a beggar. Everyone who came near him would be warned to stay away.

Naaman and his wife had tried to keep the illness a secret, but soon this was no longer possible. The secret had become known— even the maid was aware of the shocking situation.

She had not become bitter because of her captivity. Her faith in God, learned in her parents' home, had kept her from that. She submitted to her superiors and found herself sympathetic to them. They, recognizing this, confided in her.

Yes, they had a problem. But didn't problems exist so that they could be taken to God? Didn't these Syrians know that God had a

1. Leviticus 13:45,46

servant on earth—Elisha? He was a greatly honored figure in her parental home. So she came to her mistress with a very natural proposal, "Why doesn't my lord go visit the prophet who is in Samaria? He can cure him of his leprosy."

Just a few words, but what a difference they made. Instead of certain death, there was a possibility of life! Her mistress took her words seriously, and her master thought they were important enough to pass on to the king. The king ordered immediate action. As soon as possible Naaman was on his way, bearing many gifts, to see the prophet Elisha in Samaria.

When Naaman returned he was not only healed of the dreaded disease—his skin clean and without spot, looking like the healthy skin of a young boy—but the healing process had gone far deeper. His heart had been touched. He now had confidence in the God of Israel. He said, "I know that there is no God in all the earth but in Israel." Instead of worshipping idols, he became a worshipper of the living God.

Nothing more is said about the young girl whose life was described in two sentences. Yet some aspects of her life are striking.

First, she must have been an excellent servant who did her work well. Someone has said, "Your actions speak so loudly that I cannot hear what you are saying." She lived too early in history to have read James' words that a person's faith is proven by his deeds,[2] yet she practiced what James preached. Her deeds had prepared an opening for her words. She was taken seriously by her master and mistress.

Second, she did not keep silent out of shyness. She didn't think she was too young to have something significant to say.[3] She didn't feel that her position was too low for her to be heard. Instead, she saw a person in need and believed that the God of Israel could meet the need. She trusted that He would heal Naaman of his terrible disease. That was all she said, a few simple words,

Nearly 900 years later Jesus told His disciples that they would be witnesses of Him. To witness means to tell others of personal experiences, what a person has heard or seen (I John 1:2,3). In order to do that he must begin in "Jerusalem." This means to begin in his own environment. If anyone is willing to do that, then God will use the words. He blesses them. A person who is willing to witness in such a manner will receive opportunities he never would have dreamed of.

2. James 2:14,26
3. I Timothy 4:12

but the result was significant. A whole new future opened up to Naaman.

A few simple words brought new life to a man, hope for his family and support for his king. A few simple words gave attention and brought honor to the God of Israel. This little maid continues to speak to people today through the words which were recorded through the guidance of the Holy Spirit long after she died. History can never blot out what she said and did.

She didn't say much, but what she said revealed her faith—a faith that was tested by reality and a faith that served the people around her. Because of her faith a life was changed. The insignificant little maid was not so insignificant!

The Jewish maid, a girl who talked about God
(II Kings 5:1-5, 14,15; Acts 1:8)

Questions:
1. What does the Bible say about this girl? How did she arrive in Naaman's home?
2. What does the Bible tell about Naaman and his disease? Why was it so terrible? (Leviticus 13:45,46)
3. What do you conclude from the words the maid spoke to Naaman's wife?
4. What different things happened as a result of those few words?
5. What do you consider to be the most important result of her boldness?
6. Compare what the girl did with the commission Jesus gave in Acts 1:8.What lessons did you draw personally from her boldness? How are you going to apply them?

13

"In 1959 Shah Mohammed Riza Pahlavi of Persia married Farah Diba, a modern 21-year-old student. In 1967 he crowned her his empress to express in 'an unusual way' his gratitude for her part in the social and economic advancements of the country during that eight-year period. The dedication of a young woman proves again to be of far-reaching influence in Persia."

The author

Esther,
a queen who risked her life for her people

Esther 4:1,5-16 When Mordecai learned all that had been done, he tore his clothes, put on sackcloth and ashes, and went out into the midst of the city and wailed loudly and bitterly . . . . Then Esther summoned Hathach from the king's eunuchs whom the king had appointed to attend her and ordered him to go to Mordecai to learn what this was and why it was. So Hathach went out to Mordecai to the city square in front of the king's gate. And Mordecai told him all that had happened to him, and the exact amount of money that Haman had promised to pay to the king's treasuries for the destruction of the Jews. He also gave him a copy of the text of the edict which had been issued in Susa for their destruction that he might show Esther and inform her, and to order her to go in to the king to implore his favor and to plead with him for her people.

And Hathach came back and related Mordecai's words to Esther. Then Esther spoke to Hathach and ordered him to reply to Mordecai: "All the king's servants and the people of the king's provinces know that for any man or woman who comes to the king to the inner court who is not summoned, he has but one law, that he be put to death; unless the king holds out to him the golden scepter so that he may live. And I have not been summoned to come to the king for these thirty days." And they related Esther's words to Mordecai.

Then Mordecai told them to reply to Esther, "Do not imagine that you in the king's palace can escape any more than all the Jews. For if you remain silent at this time, relief and deliverance will arise for the Jews from another place and you and your father's house will perish. And who knows whether you have not attained royalty for such a time as this?" Then Esther told them to reply to Mordecai, "Go, assemble all the Jews who are found in Susa, and fast for me; do not eat or drink for three days, night or day. I and my maidens also will fast in the same way. And thus I will go in to the king, which is not according to the law; and if I perish, I perish."

Esther 7:1-6 Now the king and Haman came to drink wine with Esther the queen. And the king said to Esther on the second day also as they drank their wine at the banquet, "What is your petition, Queen Esther? It shall be granted you. And what is your request? Even to half of the kingdom it shall be done." Then Queen Esther answered and said, "If I have found favor in your sight, O king, and if it please the king, let my life be given me as my petition, and my people as my request; for we have been sold, I and my people, to be destroyed, to be killed and to be annihilated. Now if we had only been sold as slaves, men and women, I would have remained silent, for the trouble would not be commensurate with the annoyance to the king." Then King Ahasuerus asked Queen Esther, "Who is he, and where is he, who would presume to do thus?" And Esther said, "A foe and an enemy, is this wicked Haman!" Then Haman became terrified before the king and queen.

Esther 8:15-17 Then Mordecai went out from the presence of the king in royal robes of blue and white, with a large crown of gold and a garment of fine linen and purple; and the city of Susa shouted and rejoiced. For the Jews there was light and gladness and joy and honor. And in each and every province, and in each and every city, wherever the king's commandment and his decree arrived there was gladness and joy for the Jews, a feast and a holiday. And many among the peoples of the land became Jews, for the dread of the Jews had fallen on them.

The story of Queen Esther is remarkable. It has the fairy tale atmosphere of the 1,001 nights mixed with the scorching smell of Hitler's gas chambers. And while the name of God doesn't appear once in the book of Esther, His presence is evident on every page.

Esther appeared on the scene after another woman, Queen Vashti, had disappeared behind the royal backdrop. Esther was the wife of the immensely rich Persian king, Ahasuerus, who ruled over 127 provinces from India to Ethiopia in 475 B.C. His winter palace was in Susa, nearly 200 miles east of Babylon. It had floors and pillars of marble, hung with white, green and blue curtains which were held back with cords of fine linen. The royal family and their guests reclined on couches of gold and silver. During feasts they drank from vessels of gold, no two of which were alike.

Esther, a beautiful young woman with a disposition to match, had won the hearts of the royal household. She was not a Persian, but a Jewish orphan who had been raised by her cousin Mordecai, an exile from Jerusalem. He cared for her as her father would have and she obeyed him like a daughter, even though she was the queen.

Mordecai, who served the royal court, was hated by the king's chancellor, Haman, an Amalekite. Haman was brilliant, ambitious and rude. He spared no one. However, the king respected him highly and ordered all servants at the royal court to bow down before him. Mordecai was the only person who refused to do this. Because he was a Jew, the only person he would bow before was God. Haman was so embittered by this rejection that he decided to kill Mordecai and all other Jews in the great Persian empire.

He conceived a scheme so subtle and watertight that no Jew would be able to escape. All would be caught in the net he was spreading. The total annihilation of the Jews—God's people—was announced. The king's signature had made it possible for Haman to wipe them off the globe forever. Royal couriers took the fastest animals and rushed to every corner of the immense empire to announce the coming calamity. The Jews were appalled and terrified.

Esther had been married for five years. At the request of Mordecai she had remained silent about her Jewish heritage but he kept her informed daily of the situation. With the grim extinction of the Jews in sight, Mordecai felt that the only solution was for Esther to intervene.

"Go to your husband the king and ask for his help to save your people," he ordered Esther. Your people! That meant she must reveal her Jewish origin. How would the king react? Would he feel she had deceived him? Did he hate her race as Haman and many others hated it?

There was another obstacle. No one was allowed to present himself to the king without being summoned, not even the queen. To do so would mean risking her life. She had no guarantee that he still loved her as before. Maybe another woman had taken her place.

She told Mordecai that she hadn't been called to the king for thirty days. He was relentless, telling her she was the only one who could intervene. "Don't think that you will escape death. It doesn't matter that you are the queen. Every Jew will die, young boys and grey-haired men. No women or children will be spared," he said. "If you hold your peace at this time, then relief and deliverance will come to the Jews from another source, but you and your father's house will be destroyed. And who knows but you have come to the kingdom for such a time as this?"

"From another source . . . " Mordecai was thinking about God. God would not allow this impudent murder of the Jewish nation. Throughout the ages He had promised the Messiah would come through this people. Haman could not prevent this. Neither could Satan. Though the need for deliverance was immediate, Mordecai's trust in God was solid.

God's counterattack was ready. He did not execute it by a supernatural intervention. No miracle of nature,[1] no angel,[2] would save His people. Instead, a weak woman would. The future of God's people had seldom hung on such a thin thread. Would this plan succeed? Would the queen cooperate with God's plan or would she fail?

"God is looking for an instrument, Esther, a human being. Are you willing to give your life? He placed you in this strategic position long before, for He knew of the coming catastrophe. God's solution is you."

Esther didn't receive God's message through the imposing words of an established prophet, who said, "Thus says the Lord." She received no heavenly vision. She was led by the words of a

1. Exodus 14:21-30
2. Numbers 20:16

relative. God's leading could not have been more inauspicious. Yet she accepted Mordecai's words as the words of God.

Young Esther, who had always presented a mild manner, now proved that she was made of the fiber of heroes. This crisis situation revealed the power of her life—God. She was willing to subject her life to His plans. She desired to do His will. "Call all the Jews in Susa together," she said, "and let them fast with me and my maids for three days and three nights."

She was now publicly identifying herself with her people. Her call to fasting was a call to prayer.[3] She realized she was a powerless woman, that she had no help to offer. Help could only come from the Lord, the God of Israel. Therefore, she planned to assail His heavenly throne with prayer for three days and nights. Esther was deeply aware of her need for God's guidance. She wanted assurance that the requested task was appointed by Him. She knew that God revealed Himself in answer to prayer and she needed wisdom and courage to act properly. Whom should she ask for advice except the One who was the Source of all wisdom and who distributed it in answer to prayer?

"Then in spite of the law, I will go to the king. And if I die, I die." She had burned her bridges behind her. This young woman was willing to risk her position, her life and her future for her people.

After the days of prayer Esther groomed herself meticulously and went to the king, who was apparently taken up with the affairs of the kingdom. When he saw Esther his heart was touched. He held out his golden scepter to her as proof that her life was safe. He asked, "What is your request, Queen Esther? It will be granted to you."

The first part of her prayer had been answered. Her life was spared. And God had set ajar the door of salvation for her people. She had not prayed for wisdom in vain, however. She sensed that this was neither the time nor the place for her urgent request. Her insight into this situation reveals that she was a wise woman in control of her emotions and one who didn't need to make hasty decisions. She was also a woman who realized very practically that the way to a man's heart is often through his stomach. She invited the king to a meal—along with Haman.

During that meal the king asked her again, "What is your

3. Ezra 8:23; Daniel 9:3

request? I will grant it to you." Esther moved carefully, step by step, waiting upon God. In her heart she felt that she still needed to gain time. It was not yet God's time. "Come back together tomorrow," she requested. And that proved to be God's leading.

That night the king could not sleep. A courtier read to him from the book of the chronicles of his people. Important facts which had been in the dark came into the open. They fit into the jigsaw puzzle of God's plan. Recently Mordecai had revealed a conspiracy against the king and, thus, saved the king's life. But Mordecai had never been rewarded. This negligence must be corrected. Haman, the man who had erected an 83-foot high gallows near his house with the intention of hanging Mordecai, was ordered to reward him.

The following day during the meal Esther revealed her request. Touchingly, she pleaded with the king for the lives of her people. And for her own life, "If we had only been sold into slavery, I would have held my tongue," she said.

But it was not just the lives of the Jews that hung in the balance, the well-being of the king was also at stake. A consequence far worse than losing his servants and far worse than the chain-reaction of hatred against him would occur—he would be turning against God. God had called this people the apple of His eye,[4] and He would protect and keep them. No one could harm this race without risking His wrath.[5] Not even a king. Therefore, she wanted to protect him. Her insight and approach demanded the king's respect. She succeeded in convincing him. "Who is the man and where is he who would presume in his heart to do such a thing?" was the king's startling response.

Esther's finger pointed to Haman, his fellow guest and most outstanding subject. "That wicked man there—Haman," replied Esther.

Then everything came to light. The gallows that had been erected near Haman's house waited for the execution of Mordecai, but the king changed this plan. "Hang Haman on the gallows that he has erected for Mordecai," the king commanded. It was done.

Haman's wife and his wise friends had been right. They had told him, "If this Mordecai is a Jew, you cannot prevail against him. On the contrary, you will surely fall before him." It would have been

4. Deuteronomy 32:10
5. Zechariah 2:8,9

wise if Haman had learned from the history of his ancestors, the Amalekites. God was against them because they were against His people.[6] Haman found that hatred is a very dangerous emotion, one that usually turns against the one who unleashes it.

Esther had saved not only her life but also the lives of her entire race. The New Testament says that Christians should shine like lights in this world, like bright stars in the night.[7] Esther was such a star, which is precisely the meaning of her name, "star."

The words of her husband to annihilate the Jews were so mighty that they could not simply be withdrawn. A contradictory order was necessary. "Write whatever pleases you concerning the Jews," the king said to her. "I will sign it and seal it with my ring."

The heroine who had saved the Jews by risking her own life received the privilege of telling them this wonderful news! Instead of being a woman behind the scenes she had become someone of importance. Her words would weigh heavily from then on.

The good news arrived before the date of the mass slaughter. God saw to that. The day Haman had marked on the calendar to be a day of sorrow was one of joy. Many non-Jews became Jews because they were so deeply impressed by what had happened. They wanted to be on the side of the Lord.

The day of gladness became a day of commemoration. The feast of Purim was instituted. At this feast even today, Jews all over the world remember what Queen Esther did for them. Every year when Purim is celebrated the Jews read the book of Esther. She is highly respected. The Talmud even seems to prefer this book above the Psalms and the Prophets.

Thirty years later Nehemiah would rebuild the walls of Jerusalem. Without Queen Esther this would have been impossible. It is difficult to imagine the course of history without her. Humanly speaking, if there had been no Esther, there would be no Jewish nation. And without the nation, there would not have been a Messiah. And without the Messiah, the world would be lost.

Esther paved the way, unknown to her, for the coming Christ. Through her God has also indicated that His guidance is available to His followers for making decisions. These decisions should be based upon the Word of God,[8] tested by prayer[9] and the counsel of

6. Exodus 17:8-16; Deuteronomy 25:17-19   8. John 14:21

7. Philippians 2:15   9. James 1:5

others,[10] dependent upon an inner assurance[11] and upon God-opened doors.[12]

Esther, a queen who risked her life for her people
(Esther 4:1,5-16; 7:1-6; 8:15-17)

Questions:
1. What most impressed you about the character and life attitude of Esther?
2. Repeat in your own words the content of Esther 4:14.
3. Consider her call to fasting in light of Ezra 8:23 and Daniel 9:3. What can you learn from this?
4. What is the proof that Esther purposely risked her life for her people?
5. Describe what happened to her people as a result of her intervention.
6. Study Esther's dedication in light of Ezekiel 22:30. What are your conclusions?
7. What has this story taught you about God's leading?

10. Proverbs 15:22
11. I John 3:21   12. Revelation 3:7,8

14

"The main guilt of a man are not his sins. Temptation is powerful and his strength is weak. The main guilt of a man is that he can turn any moment to God and neglects to do that." *

Job's wife,
the woman who said no to God

Job 1:1-3,6-12 There was a man in the land of Uz, whose name was Job, and that man was blameless, upright, fearing God, and turning away from evil. And seven sons and three daughters were born to him. His possessions also were 7,000 sheep, 3,000 camels, 500 yoke of oxen, 500 female donkeys, and very many servants; and that man was the greatest of all the men of the east . . .

Now there was a day when the sons of God came to present themselves before the Lord, Satan also came among them. And the Lord said to Satan, "From where do you come?" Then Satan answered the Lord and said, "From roaming about on the earth and walking around on it." And the Lord said to Satan, "Have you considered My servant Job? For there is no one like him on the earth, a blameless and upright man, fearing God and turning away from evil." Then Satan answered the Lord, "Does Job fear God for nothing? Hast Thou not made a hedge about him and his house and all that he has, on every side? Thou hast blessed the work of his hands, and his possessions have increased in the land. But put forth Thy hand now and touch all that he has; he will surely curse Thee to Thy face." Then the Lord said to Satan, "Behold, all that he has is in your power, only do not put forth your hand on him." So Satan departed from the presence of the Lord.

*Boenam, Rabbi and Buber, Martin. *Fountains of Jewish Wisdom,* © 1969, Leobuchhandlung, Sankt Gallen, Switzerland.

Job 2:1-10 Again there was a day when the sons of God came to present themselves before the Lord, and Satan also came among them to present himself before the Lord. And the Lord said to Satan, "Where have you come from?" Then Satan answered the Lord and said, "From roaming about on the earth, and walking around on it." And the Lord said to Satan, "Have you considered My servant Job? For there is no one like him on the earth, a blameless and upright man fearing God and turning away from evil. And he still holds fast his integrity, although you incited Me against him, to ruin him without cause." And Satan answered the Lord and said, "Skin for skin! Yes, all that a man has he will give for his life. However, put forth Thy hand, now, and touch his bone and his flesh; he will curse Thee to Thy face." So the Lord said to Satan, "Behold, he is in your power only spare his life." Then Satan went out from the presence of the Lord, and smote Job with sore boils from the sole of his foot to the crown of his head. And he took a potsherd to scrape himself while he was sitting among the ashes. Then his wife said to him, "Do you still hold fast your integrity? Curse God and die!" But he said to her, "You speak as one of the foolish women speaks. Shall we indeed accept good from God and not accept adversity?" In all this Job did not sin with his lips.

Job 42:10-13 And the Lord restored the fortunes of Job when he prayed for his friends, and the Lord increased all that Job had twofold. Then all his brothers, and all his sisters, and all who had known him before, came to him, and they ate bread with him in his house; and they consoled him and comforted him for all the evil that the Lord had brought on him. And each one gave him one piece of money, and each a ring of gold. And the Lord blessed the latter days of Job more than his beginning, and he had 14,000 sheep, and 6,000 camels, and 1,000 yoke of oxen, and 1,000 female donkeys. And he had seven sons and three daughters.

Romans 8:28 And we know that God causes all things to work together for good to those who love God, to those who are called according to His purpose.

The wife of Job lived in the land of Uz, in Arabia, probably not far from Ur of the Chaldeans, the city where God called Abraham. Few women were as privileged as she was. Her husband was immensely rich. Their royal household contained many servants. She had seven sons and three daughters. They were all wealthy and had pleasant, frequent meetings with one another. They even conducted regular family parties to strengthen their mutual bond. But the greatest of her blessings was her husband, Job.

Job was a man who loved God. All he knew about God was what others had told him, but that was sufficient to cause Job to serve Him devotedly. The depth of Job's spiritual life accounted for the warm atmosphere in their home. His life was so permeated by this God-centered devotion that people around him were aware of it. People said that Job was a devout man and that this was the reason he was prosperous. The foundation of Job's wife's life was the piety and prosperity of her husband and household—

This was the situation on earth.

Something remarkable took place in heaven at this time. Job was the subject of a conversation between God and Satan. God was pleased that Job, a man on earth, loved Him voluntarily. God was looking for people like Job—he was fulfilling the purpose for which God had created him—fellowship with Himself.

Satan, the accuser of believers,[1] didn't agree with God's evaluation of Job. He contradicted what people on earth were saying about Job. He felt that the reason Job was devout was that he was prosperous and suggested that if prosperity was withheld from Job that he would turn from God.

"All right," replied God. "We'll test your accusation, Satan. Take his possessions from him, but do not harm him."

Satan was devilishly happy with this arrangement and poured calamities upon Job like unexpected showers in March. One terrible blow after another befell him. His enormous stock of cattle was either stolen or struck by lightning. Thus Job lost all his wealth. But the greatest catastrophe of all Satan reserved until last—he destroyed all of Job's children.

Everything Job had built over many years was gone in one blow. The richest man in the entire East was suddenly bereft and without children. All that was left to him, besides his home, were four servants—and his wife.

Satan had done his work thoroughly, but he still hadn't achieved

1. Revelation 12:9,10

his purpose. Although Job, like a man of the East, did rend his garments, his faith in God remained unshaken. "I was born with nothing, and when I die I will have nothing; the Lord gave, and the Lord has taken away; blessed be the name of the Lord," said Job.[2]

Satan and God talked once again about Job. God pointed out Job's continued loyalty. Satan reacted by saying that Job hadn't been harmed personally. Only his possessions and externals had been affected. Let him touch his body and then see if his faith would still stand.

God then allowed Satan to do what he wished with the single restriction that he could not take Job's life. Satan sent a disease so terrible it could drive a man out of his mind. Job was covered from the soles of his feet to the top of his head with itching, sore boils.

Medical science agrees that the suffering of such a patient would be unbearable—beyond one's imagination. The hideous disease drove him to the dung pit, where dogs rummaged for cadavers of animals and where the lowest of humans searched for what others had thrown away. There he sat and scraped his sores with a piece of broken pottery—

But then came the greatest blow of all. His wife turned against him. The woman God had intended to support Job for better or for worse, the woman he needed now more than ever before, no longer supported him. Through her Satan played his last card. "Do you still retain your integrity?" she asked bitterly. "Curse God and die!"

She was so overcome by sorrow that she was only able to see one way out—to renounce faith in God and commit suicide. Her reaction was just the opposite of her husband's.

Job's faith endured even this crisis. The true situation may have been hidden from him, but he did not doubt God. God was still a reality to him. Therefore, he was able to accept both the good and the bad from Him. His life was built on a rock and although storms beat against it incessantly, it wouldn't collapse. It was a foundation that would last.

As the roots of a tree are tested for strength in a storm, so the storms of sorrow and unexplainable experiences uncover the life

2. Job 1:21

foundation of a man. Job had a strong foundation; his wife did not. Naturally, her sorrows were extreme. It is hard to identify with her loss. She could have sustained herself if she had built her life on the same solid foundation as her husband. But their different responses to the situation were not due to the way they each experienced the

Many centuries later, after the Redeemer in whom Job believed came (Job 19:25), died, rose from the dead and ascended into heaven, Paul wrote that there is only one foundation on which a man can build his life—Jesus Christ (I Corinthians 3:11).

sorrow, but to their foundation.[3] Thus, she was unable to support her husband during the most difficult period of his life.

At least Job's friends came to visit him, though they were of no help. But, the Bible doesn't record any attempts on the part of his wife to soften his pain. During the entire period of suffering she was never in the foreground of the story.

God has entrusted women with a unique talent to sympathize and to encourage others. But Job's wife didn't use it when he needed it most.

Suddenly and radically the situation changed again. Job and his wife again had ten children, seven sons and three daughters as before. His livestock was restored; in fact, he had even more cattle than before the catastrophe.

But Job's suffering had born fruit far more important than these temporal things. His relationship with God had been deepened. "I had heard about You before," Job told God, "but now I have seen You."[4]

No longer did Job need to rely upon the experience of others, for he had met God personally. This led him to repentance and humility.[5] These two characteristics are inevitable results from a meeting with God.

Job had received insight into himself and God. He understood that there needed to be a Mediator between God and man.[6] Thus the suffering had served a positive function for him. It had revealed to Job things he had never known before. Like Jacob he had wrestled with God and prevailed.[7] The result was a richer and happier life.

And Satan? He was the loser again. The result of his tempting

3. Matthew 7:24-27
4. Job 42:5
5. Job 42:6
6. Job 9:32-35; 16:19
7. Genesis 32:28

Job was exactly the opposite of what he had planned—Job was more dedicated to God than ever.

The Bible does not say much about Job's wife. It states that in the heat of the temptation she had pointed to the wrong party— God—as being guilty. Like many unbelievers she had been blinded by Satan.[8] She failed to understand that although God allows suffering, His aim is not merely that man should suffer, but that suffering should bear positive fruit.[9] Her fragile happiness had been taken from her temporarily in order for her to find the unchangeable happiness—God Himself. The road to finding this happiness, however, ran through the school of suffering.

As an Old Testament woman she naturally carried a doubly heavy load. She missed the encouragement of the written Word of God and she had no circle of Christian friends to support her. Yet she had living proof that it was not necessary to be defeated in a crisis, not even in her day. Her husband, Job, was that proof. The New Testament praises him because he continued to trust in God in times of sorrow.[10] When Satan aimed his fiery arrows of temptation Job used his faith like a shield, stopping them.[11]

He proved that no man is tempted so strongly that he cannot stand up against it and that God does show a way to escape in the midst of every temptation.[12]

Job had built his life upon God's foundation. But it appears that his wife could find no solid ground for her feet. Sorrow threw Job into the arms of God. But, in the critical hour of her life, Job's wife said no to God. That doesn't make her a good example to follow.

Job's wife, the woman who said no to God
(Job 1:1-3, 6-12; 2:1-10; 42:10-13; Romans 8:28)

Questions:
1. Describe Job's family before the catastrophies.
2. Who was the cause of the sorrow that afflicted Job's family? (See also Revelation 12:9,10.)

8. II Corinthians 4:4,11
9. Hebrews 12:11   11. Ephesians 6:16
10. James 5:11   12. I Corinthians 10:13

3. Reflect upon the reaction of Job's wife. Formulate her response in your own words.
4. Look at her life and her husband's life in regard to Matthew 7:24-27. What can you conclude?
5. What encouragement does the Bible offer to Christians who persevere in difficulties? Compare James 5:11, Hebrews 12:11 and I Corinthians 10:13.
6. What did you personally learn from the experiences of Job's wife? What are you doing to apply this to your own life?

15

"My heart is overflowing with praise of my Lord,
my soul is full of joy in God my Saviour.
For He has deigned to notice me, His humble servant
and all generations to come will call me the happiest
of women!" Mary*

Mary,
the most privileged among women

Luke 1:26-38 Now in the sixth month the angel Gabriel was sent from God to a city in Galilee, called Nazareth, to a virgin engaged to a man whose name was Joseph, of the descendants of David; and the virgin's name was Mary. And coming in, he said to her, "Hail, favored one! The Lord is with you." But she was greatly troubled at this statement, and kept pondering what kind of salutation this might be. And the angel said to her, "Do not be afraid, Mary; for you have found favor with God. And behold, you will conceive in your womb, and bear a son, and you shall name Him Jesus. He will be great, and will be called the Son of the Most High; and the Lord God will give Him the throne of His father David; and He will reign over the house of Jacob forever; and His kingdom will have no end." And Mary said to the angel, "How can this be, since I am a virgin?" And the angel answered and said to her, "The Holy Spirit will come upon you, and the power of the Most High will overshadow you; and for that reason the holy offspring shall be called the Son of God. And behold, even your relative Elizabeth has also conceived a son in her old age; and she who was called barren is now in her sixth month. For nothing will be impossible with God." And Mary said, "Behold, the bondslave of the Lord; be it done to me according to your word." And the angel departed from her.

*Luke 1:46b-48. Phillips, J. B. *The New Testament in Modern English,*
© 1972, The Macmillan Company, New York, N.Y.

Matthew 1:18-25 Now the birth of Jesus Christ was as follows. When His mother Mary had been betrothed to Joseph, before they came together she was found to be with child by the Holy Spirit. And Joseph her husband, being a righteous man, and not wanting to disgrace her, desired to put her away secretly. But when he had considered this, behold, an angel of the Lord appeared to him in a dream, saying, "Joseph, son of David, do not be afraid to take Mary as your wife; for that which has been conceived in her is of the Holy Spirit. And she will bear a Son; and you shall call His name Jesus, for it is He who will save His people from their sins." Now all this took place that what was spoken by the Lord through the prophet might be fulfilled, saying, *"Behold, the virgin shall be with child, and shall bear a Son, and they shall call His name Immanuel,"* which translated means, *"God with us."* And Joseph arose from his sleep, and did as the angel of the Lord commanded him, and took her as his wife, and kept her a virgin until she gave birth to a Son; and he called His name Jesus.

Luke 2:6-14 And it came about that while they were there, the days were completed for her to give birth. And she gave birth to her first-born Son; and she wrapped Him in cloths, and laid Him in a manger, because there was no room for them in the inn.

And in the same region there were some shepherds staying out in the fields, and keeping watch over their flock by night. And an angel of the Lord suddenly stood before them, and the glory of the Lord shone around them; and they were terribly frightened. And the angel said to them, "Do not be afraid; for behold, I bring you good news of a great joy which shall be for all the people; for today in the city of David there has been born for you a Saviour, who is Christ the Lord. And this will be a sign for you: you will find a Baby wrapped in cloths, and lying in a manger." And suddenly there appeared with the angel a multitude of the heavenly host praising God, and saying, "Glory to God in the highest, and on earth peace among men with whom He is pleased."

Luke 2:17-19 And when they had seen this, they made known the statement which had been told them about this Child. And all who heard it wondered at the things which were told them by the shepherds. But Mary treasured up all these things, pondering them in her heart.

Luke 2:33-35 And His father and mother were amazed at the things which were being said about Him. And Simeon blessed them, and said to Mary His mother, "Behold, this Child is appointed for the fall and rise of many in Israel, and for a sign to be opposed—and a sword will pierce even your own soul—to the end that thoughts from many hearts may be revealed."

John 19:25-27 Therefore the soldiers did these things. But there were standing by the Cross of Jesus His mother, and His mother's sister, Mary the wife of Clopas, and Mary Magdalene. When Jesus therefore saw His mother, and the disciple whom He loved standing nearby, He said to His mother, "Woman, behold, your son!" Then He said to the disciple, "Behold, your mother!" And from that hour the disciple took her into his own household.

"I am the Lord's servant and I will do whatever He desires," she stammered, totally overwhelmed by the message the angel had just brought. In her thoughts she reviewed what he had said. She, Mary, would become the mother of the Messiah! The Redeemer who had been promised first to Adam, then more clearly to Abraham and was later foretold by various prophets, would be brought into the world by her.

She realized that He would be coming. Every Jewish woman had hoped it would be her privilege to be the mother of the Messiah. And now His time had come—and she had been chosen to be His mother. She had never dreamed she would be the one.

She was young and she came from a very insignificant village.[1] And—how could she give birth to a baby? Why she wasn't even married! She was only engaged. It is no wonder she replied, "But I am a virgin and not even married. How can this happen?"

The angel had begun with, "Don't be afraid, Mary, for God has chosen to bless you." Then he had told her how the Holy Spirit would work this miracle in her. Her Child would be called the Son of God.

Mary knew God, through the books of Moses, the Psalms and the writings of the prophets. She had a deep reverence for the Lord God in her heart because she knew what He had done in the history of her people. She was aware of what He had done not only for the entire nation but for certain individuals.

---

1. John 1:46,47

She knew of His graciousness toward those who reverenced Him and that He preferred to work through those who had no worldly might. She was well aware of the fact that she had no position or wealth. Was that the reason that He had selected her? Was she a usable instrument because she could claim no worldly honor in and of herself?

Mary was willing to sacrifice herself to become His lowliest servant. "May everything you said come true," she said simply, gazing at the departing angel.

These words indicated complete surrender on her part. She was not holding anything back.

It was not an ill-considered answer. Her Son, the One who had just been announced, would utter practically the same words in Gethsemane, "Not My will, but Your will be done."[2] In the future she would have ample opportunity to prove that she meant just what she said. However, at that moment she could not foresee the consequences.

Mary, the most privileged among women, learned from the very beginning that exceptional privilege often goes hand in hand with sacrifice. Moses had experienced this before her.[3] Paul would after her.[4]

The first thing she sacrificed was her reputation. She exchanged this in order to be available to God. This created a problem for Joseph, her fiance. He was a man who walked with God. How could he possibly marry a girl who was expecting a baby by someone else?

Because he loved her, he didn't want to accuse her openly, for if he did, and that was what the Law expected of him, Mary would be put to death. The Law stated that if a Hebrew bride had betrayed her husband, and was not a virgin at marriage, she was to be stoned without pardon.[5]

Therefore, Joseph planned to leave her quietly. Did he want to give the problem of what should happen to her back to God? If so, he would be putting the problem back where it belonged.

In a dream the angel of the Lord disclosed the true nature of the situation to Joseph. Mary was pregnant with the promised Emmanuel about whom Isaiah had prophesied.[6]

2. Matthew 26:39
3. Hebrews 11:24-26
4. Acts 9:15,16
5. Deuteronomy 22:20,21
6. Isaiah 7:14

Joseph would also be a privileged person as the Child's earthly father. He would be the one to give the Child His name, Jesus. It was to be his honor to educate the Child, as if He were his own son. Joseph's house was to be the house where the Son of God, during His time on earth, would feel most comfortable. For Jesus, it was to be His only earthly home.

Joseph married Mary. He had to sacrifice some personal happiness in exchange for the honor bestowed on him. Not only was he marrying a woman whose purity was questioned by those around them, he was to have no sexual relations with her until after Jesus was born.

Together Joseph and Mary climbed the steps of the Temple Square in Jerusalem. They carried the Child and a pair of turtledoves to offer to the Lord.

Mary thought over the past year's events. She remembered how, soon after the visit of the angel Gabriel, she had gone to a small village near Jerusalem to visit her relative Elizabeth, who had also been expecting a baby.

Without her mentioning a word about her own pregnancy Elizabeth had welcomed her as blessed among women. Filled with the Holy Spirit, Elizabeth had called her "the mother of my Lord."

Mary recalled her own reaction. It had been a burst of praise to God, a song of praise that He had put in her heart. She had been deeply impressed by the magnitude of the things that were going to happen. People would call her blessed throughout future generations. Not because of herself, but because of what God had done. He was great, holy and almighty. She was unworthy of this. She had nothing to offer but her gratitude and praise. The Child to be born would also be her Saviour. Though she felt privileged, she also realized that she too was a sinner who needed the Saviour.

Mary's humility can be seen in her deeply impressive Magnificat—her praise to God (Luke 1:46-55). She could not have known that even after many centuries people would still be moved and stimulated by her love for God.

When the delivery of the Child was at hand, Caesar Augustus had ordered a census to be taken throughout the nation. Mary and Joseph had made the long journey from Nazareth to Bethlehem, the ancient home of King David, forefather of them both, to be registered. As they had expected, every inn was full. Bethlehem, situated on the caravan route from Jerusalem to Hebron, was a very busy city.

Her Child had been born outside the city in a cave where farm animals were kept in the winter. She was sad that her Son didn't even have a bed to sleep on His first night on earth.

While she and Joseph had been alone and lonely, a miracle had occurred. A bright light shown in the night—a light brighter than day. Suddenly a great army of angels had appeared. "Glory to God in the highest heaven, and peace on earth . . ." they had sung, as they proclaimed the birth of God's Son, the Saviour of the world.

Shepherds, appointed by the angels, had come to the stable. They were poor men with weather-beaten faces. Later, rich and learned men came from the East. They had made a long journey to bring honor and precious gifts of gold, frankincense and costly oil. In this way her Son had been announced by God and welcomed by rich and poor alike.[7]

She sat quietly, not knowing quite what to say, her heart absorbed in all these precious memories.

Suddenly as they carried their Son into the Temple a very old man approached them and took the Child from them.[8] The old man was Simeon, a devout man, who had been waiting for the coming of the Messiah for a long time. "You have kept Your promise, Lord. Now You may let Your servant go in peace," they heard him say, much to their amazement. He continued, "For I have seen Him as You promised I would. I have seen the Saviour You have given to the world."

The old man's speech had been guided by the Holy Spirit. There was no longer any question in the minds of Joseph and Mary that they were holding the Son of God in their arms.

Anna, an elderly prophetess, who had, like Simeon, spent most of her adult life in the presence of God, also recognized the Child as the promised Messiah.

Before Anna left for the city to tell the people that the redemption of Jerusalem was at hand, Simeon said something remarkable to Mary, "Listen carefully, this Child shall be rejected by many in Israel, but He will be of the greatest joy to many others.

7. Matthew 2:1-12
8. Luke 2:22-38

The deepest thoughts of many hearts shall be revealed, but a sword shall pierce your soul."

It wasn't long before the first sorrow came. King Herod had all boys two years and younger in Bethlehem murdered hoping to kill the announced King of the Jews.[9] Joseph and his little family escaped because they had been warned by God. They were forced, however, to take a long trip through the inhospitable Negev Desert, a country virtually without food and water. What made this journey to Egypt even more difficult for Mary was the knowledge that many children were being murdered because of her Son. In her mind she heard the cries of the innocent babies who were being brutally slaughtered. Being a new mother herself, she easily identified with the pain of the mothers of those children. The mother of the Son of God was finding that great joy was mingled with many tears.

Ten years had passed.
It was very crowded and busy in Jerusalem. Entire families were there to celebrate the feast of the Passover in the Holy City and to honor the Lord God with sacrifices.[10]
It was a happy occasion for they were able to worship the Lord in the company of old friends they only met on such festive days. Because of the large number of families visiting the city, it was teeming with children.
The adults enjoyed their too rare contact with relatives and friends from far away. They walked and talked loudly with one another in the streets. The children twittered like young birds as they danced and frolicked together. It was easy for the absence of a child to go unnoticed in such a multitude. The parents would naturally assume that the child was in the company of others somewhere else in the group.
That was why Joseph and Mary did not discover until after a full, tiring day on the homeward journey that Jesus was not with them. He was nowhere to be found. Finally, heavy-hearted, they returned to Jerusalem to search for Him.
They looked everywhere, without success.

9. Matthew 2:13-16
10. Luke 2:41-51

Finally, after three days of searching, they found Him in the Temple. To their amazement the young Jesus was seated among the highly learned rabbis. He was not just listening to them, he was asking them questions as well. He surprised them with His intelligence, understanding and properly spoken answers.

Mary was upset. "Son," she rebuked Him, "why have You done this? Your father and I have been searching for You all over Jerusalem." His answer, not unfriendly, but clear and without reserve, "You shouldn't have had to search. Didn't you know I would be in my Father's house?"

His father? But Joseph had been looking for Him everywhere along with His mother. Hadn't she understood that He was talking about His heavenly Father?

Jesus was beginning to grow away from them. He was beginning His life's journey toward His true destiny. While He was their lost son today, He was also the Son of God, the Redeemer of a lost world. The ties between Him and His family had already begun to loosen.

Did this experience remind Mary of Simeon's words? Was she experiencing the initial pains of the sword that would finally pierce her heart?

When they returned to Nazareth everything appeared to be unchanged. Jesus was obedient to them as before. But something had happened in Mary's heart. She kept this memory and recorded it with the others in her heart. She was being given the opportunity to subject her motherly desires to the will of God.

Their years together were good as Jesus grew from youth to manhood. His mother's influence upon Him during that time was great.

"Jesus grew up to be tall and wise, and both God and men loved Him."[11] Jesus, the Son of God, who was perfect as a child, developed naturally into a man. This is a holy mystery, how God as a man on earth could submit Himself to the influence of Mary.

Jesus did not grow up in a rich or socially privileged family. But His spiritual environment was enviable. Both His parents walked with God and respected one another. Mary's thoughts, especially, were full of God.

---

11. Luke 2:52

A person's thoughts determine his deeds. Following that principle, Joseph and Mary strove to make their home and the education of their children conform to the thoughts of God. There was a friendly atmosphere in that tiny home in Nazareth. It was permeated with a spirit of true humility and a natural devoutness. It was a spirit that made it easy for the children to obey their parents. It was in the home of Joseph and Mary that Jesus first encountered the Scriptures. His mother's love for the Word of God was an example to her Son.

For 18 years He lived in His parents' home.

More children were born. There were other sons—James, Joses, Simon and Judas—and daughters also.[12] Since Joseph died during this period it is very likely that Jesus, as the eldest son, shared His mother's family problems and was responsible for the family's livelihood.

People no longer called Him the carpenter's son. He was now the carpenter.[13]

When Jesus was 30 years old, everything changed. Mary saw this clearly when she attended a wedding feast with Him in Cana, a little village near Nazareth on the rolling hills of the Galilean countryside.[14] She noticed that the host was embarrassed because the wine had run out. Her first reaction was to relay the problem to her Firstborn. Then she made a painful discovery. Her Son seemed to be changed. He was not behaving like the obedient Son she knew so well. "Woman," He replied, "What do I have to do with you?" Adressing her as "woman" did not indicate a lack of respect or unfriendliness. Hebrew women were used to being addressed that way. But it clearly marked a distance between Him and His mother. *When had He ever treated me in such a manner before?* she wondered. Then her memories went back to that day in the Temple. At that time He had indicated in much the same way that He, though her Son, was not able to obey every one of her orders. He had higher orders to follow.

Mary was not touchy, and if she was uncomfortable she didn't show it. "Do whatever He tells you," she said to the servants, for she knew that He was God and could work miracles.

She seemed to be willing to take second place. Did she already

12. Matthew 13:55,56
13. Mark 6:3   14. John 2:1-11

understand that He would later be teaching about the high priority God put on serving?[15]

When His ministry began, He left Mary for good. From then on He was not primarily the Son of Mary, but Jesus of Nazareth, about whom the entire country had begun to talk, for the Son of God went around the countryside doing good.

Mary learned to draw back, yet not without pain. Increasingly she experienced the cutting edge of the sword in her life, but she also realized that her sorrow was bound up with the favor of God. All that remained for her to do was to make herself available to Him again and again.

As Jesus moved throughout the countryside, healing the sick and preaching the Gospel, Mary's faith in Him found opportunity to grow. It was no doubt painful to her that her other sons didn't believe in Him,[16] and that the people of Nazareth would not accept Him.[17] He made this painfully clear to her when she and her sons tried to talk with Him. When He was told, "Your mother and brothers are here and want You to come to them," He answered, "Who are My mother and brothers?" Then, while pointing to His disciples, He added, "The person who does God's will is My brother, and he is My sister and My mother."[18]

The men with whom He mixed daily and His followers were equal to her. Relationships were no longer tested by the bond of blood, but by the bond of shared faith in God.

The sword pierced through her soul with all of its sharpness when she stood at the foot of the Cross on which her Son hung like a common criminal.

Here Mary's suffering found its climax.

She didn't try to ignore it, or try to make it easy for herself. Like Him she also drank the bitter cup of suffering to the final drop. She was with Him till His final moment. She saw His agony and heard Him scoffed at and mocked.

The hours passed slowly in the scorching sun, and Someone— the most beloved of all—suffered as no other man can ever suffer.

Mary stood beneath the Cross and suffered with Him. This was part of motherhood. The words still echoed in her mind, "May everything you said come true." She held on only because she had

15. Matthew 23:11,12   17. Luke 4:16-30
16. John 7:3-5   18. Matthew 12:46-50

made herself totally available to the Lord. How she felt was secondary.

Jesus saw her, and though in agony of death, He did not forget to take care of her. "Woman, there is your son," she heard Him say. And then He said to John, the man He loved most on earth, "There is your mother."[19]

Jesus hadn't left His earthly life without taking good care of His mother. The man and the woman who on earth were the nearest to Him would best be able to understand and help one another after He was gone. From then on Mary lived in John's home.

The Cross is not Mary's last appearance in Scripture. She appears again with Jesus' disciples, several other women and her other sons after Christ's ascension. In the upper room in Jerusalem, Mary dedicated herself, like the others, to consistent prayer.[20]

Though she had lost her Son, she did not concern herself with her personal loss, but accepted that her task regarding Him had been fulfilled.

Mary, the woman most blessed and most privileged of all women, whose name was more greatly honored than that of any other mortal, dedicated herself anew to God. Again she had no claim. Inconspicuously, she took her place among the others. Mary knew that she could overlook personal interests and dedicated herself wholly to the honor of God.

Mary had become a mature woman. In the last thirty years of her life, she had reached unknown pinnacles of happiness. At the same time she had experienced deep heart sorrows which no other woman ever has or ever will encounter. But her attitude toward God hadn't changed. She had proven with her life that she meant the words she spoke when the Messiah was announced, "I am the Lord's servant, and I will do whatever He desires."

19. John 19:26,27
20. Acts 1:9-14

Mary, the most privileged among women
(Luke 1:26-38; Matthew 1:18-25; Luke 2:6-14, 17-19, 33-35; John
19:25-27)

Questions:
1. What made Mary the most privileged of all women?
2. Study her Magnificat (Luke 1:46-55). What were her thoughts
   about God? How did she think about herself?
3. Mary's privileged position meant making sacrifices. List the
   sacrifices she had to make.
4. What do you consider to be the most difficult thing Mary faced
   as a mother?
5. What do you consider to be Mary's most remarkable
   characteristics? Support your conclusions.
6. What is the most important thing you have learned from Mary?
   What practical value does this have for your personal life?

16

*"A capable, intelligent and virtuous woman,
who is he who can find her? She is far
more precious than jewels, and her value
is far above rubies or pearls."* Solomon*

Elizabeth,
strong of character and a good life-partner

Luke 1:5-20 In the days of Herod, king of Judea, there was a certain priest named Zacharias, of the division of Abijah; and he had a wife from the daughters of Aaron, and her name was Elizabeth. And they were both righteous in the sight of God, walking blamelessly in all the commandments and requirements of the Lord. And they had no child, because Elizabeth was barren, and they were both advanced in years.

Now it came about, while he was performing his priestly service before God in the appointed order of his division, according to the custom of the priestly office, he was chosen by lot to enter the Temple of the Lord and burn incense. And the whole multitude of the people were in prayer outside at the hour of the incense offering. And an angel of the Lord appeared to him, standing to the right of the altar of incense. And Zacharias was troubled when he saw him, and fear gripped him. But the angel said to him, "Do not be afraid, Zacharias, for your petition has been heard, and your wife Elizabeth will bear you a son, and you will give him the name John. And you will have joy and gladness, and many will rejoice at his birth. For he will be great in the sight of the Lord, and he will drink no wine or liquor; and he will be filled with the Holy Spirit, while yet in his mother's womb. And he will turn back many of the sons of

*Proverbs 31:10. *Amplified Old Testament,*
© 1962, Zondervan Publishing House, Grand Rapids, Michigan.

Israel to the Lord their God. And it is he who will go as a forerunner before Him in the spirit and power of Elijah, *To turn the hearts of the fathers back to the children,* and the disobedient to the attitude of the righteous; so as to make ready a people prepared for the Lord."

And Zacharias said to the angel, "How shall I know this for certain? For I am an old man, and my wife is advanced in years." And the angel answered and said to him, "I am Gabriel, who stands in the presence of God; and I have been sent to speak to you, and to bring you this good news. And behold, you shall be silent and unable to speak until the day when these things take place, because you did not believe my words, which shall be fulfilled in their proper time."

Luke 1:24,25 And after these days Elizabeth his wife became pregnant; and she kept herself in seclusion for five months, saying, "This is the way the Lord has dealt with me in the days when He looked with favor upon me, to take away my disgrace among men."

Luke 1:39-45 Now at this time Mary arose and went with haste to the hill country, to a city of Judah, and entered the house of Zacharias and greeted Elizabeth. And it came about that when Elizabeth heard Mary's greeting, the baby leaped in her womb; and Elizabeth was filled with the Holy Spirit. And she cried out with a loud voice, and said, "Blessed among women are you, and blessed is the fruit of your womb! And how has it happened to me, that the mother of my Lord should come to me? For behold, when the sound of your greeting reached my ears, the baby leaped in my womb for joy. And blessed is she who believed that there would be a fulfillment of what had been spoken to her by the Lord."

Elizabeth was a remarkable woman. She was the wife of a priest. Priests were only allowed to marry pious women whose moral behavior was totally blameless.[1] Otherwise they would defile their husbands' holy ministries. Elizabeth was such a woman.

She was not only married to a priest, she herself was a descendant of the distinguished tribe of Aaron. Her name was derived from the same root word as that of Aaron's wife, Elisheba.

The Bible stresses that they were both righteous before God, walking blamelessly in all the commandments and ordinances of the Lord.

---

1. Leviticus 21:1a,7

No one spoke badly of her. She didn't simply follow in the spiritual wake of her pious husband, she had an independently developed spiritual life and was honored because of her personal relationship with God.

Elizabeth lived not only to the letter of the Law, she also served God in the spirit of the Law. In light of all this, her childlessness was enigmatic and painful to her. Like Eve and every Jewish mother who had brought children into the world since, she had hoped to become the mother of the Messiah. Yet she underwent the same humiliation of being childless as any other Jewish woman from whom the blessing of children had been withheld.

Often she had asked herself the painful questions, "What have I done wrong?" and "Why is God not merciful to me—why doesn't He bless?"

She was now very old, and the much desired child had not come. Was she still expectant, even at this age? Or had she resigned herself to the thought that her prayers were not pleasing to the Lord and that she would have no children?

Did she draw courage from the lives of Sarah, Rebekah and Hannah, women who also had been without children for a long time?

Life was full of surprises, not only for the mothers of Isaac, Jacob and Samuel, women who after waiting so many years finally had great sons, but also for Elizabeth.

Her husband belonged to a group of priests who served in the house of the Lord.[2] During his six-month period of duty Zacharias had the opportunity to burn incense in the sanctuary. This was a great honor, one that a priest could receive, at most, once in his life. Many never received it. The day Zacharias burned the incense opened up a new phase of life for him and Elizabeth. As so often when heaven seems to be made of brass because no prayers get answered, everything happened at once.

Gabriel, God's special messenger, stood before the priest and said, "Don't be afraid, Zacharias. Your prayers have been heard. Your wife, Elizabeth, will bear you a son, and you shall call him John."

The long wait was being rewarded. Zacharias and Elizabeth would have a son. God was going to remove their shame. New life was coming into their quiet home. Its quietness would be banished by the tramping of the child's feet and his shouting laughter. But God had still more good news.

A new future was dawning for the entire Jewish nation!

Their son would not be like every other child. He would be a man dedicated to God, who would help his people return to God. Jesus would testify of him that no greater man ever lived.[3]

The horizon widened; the vision increased. The blessing that was to result from the birth of John would stretch far beyond the small borders of his own country and people. It would reach out to the entire world. John would be the man to prepare the way for the coming Messiah. He was the herald of the Kingdom to come.

Zacharias, your prayers have indeed been heard. Not only your prayers regarding a child, but also your prayers regarding the Messiah.

How could a human being embrace so much happiness at once?

Zacharias revealed that he couldn't. He asked for a sign, and God gave him His answer. For nine full months he could not utter a word. Everything he desired to say he had to write down.

But Elizabeth evidently had no problems in believing the fantastic promise, even though she had not received it as her husband had, directly from God through a godly messenger. She had to accept it prosaically as her husband wrote it down on a tablet.

Did Elizabeth have such a close walk with God that she could hear His voice? Or had she responded more in faith? The Bible doesn't say.

While many people in the West simply choose a baby's name for its sound or name him after a special friend, this was not true in Elizabeth's society. John's name was like a clarion call: "God is gracious!" God Himself gave this name to John. No one could have given him a more beautiful one.

Elizabeth was thinking about these things while the miracle took place within her body. She withdrew for five months. Was it because she felt ill at ease showing her growing body to the inquisitive people around her? Perhaps.

But her main reason was God. She marveled at the miracle that was taking place—not only because God proved again that He

---

3. Matthew 11:11

specializes in the impossible, but also because of His unending faithfulness.

What had seemed to be a punishment now proved to be a blessing.

God had had a very special son in mind for her and Zacharias, but they had had to wait for His timing. His time couldn't come before the birth of the Lord Jesus was at hand. She was going to bring an exceptional child into the world, a child who would have a unique place in history. She was blessed indeed.

Her patience had been greatly tested and was exceptionally rewarded.

If Elizabeth did react more spiritually than her husband to the news, there is no evidence of any self-exaltation. Nor did she look down on him. She didn't move him down in order to move herself up. Rather, she responded like a good wife who accepts weakness in her life-partner.

Elizabeth not only had a distinguished background, she had a distinguished and independent character, in the positive sense of this word. When their son was born the relatives and neighbors interfered—trying to force the tradition of giving the child his father's name.

Elizabeth refused this choice.

She would not give in to conforming pressure, but remained loyal to her husband and to God. Firmly and resolutely, she said, "His name will be John."

Her life was characterized by other virtues, such as humility and modesty. These were evident in an outstanding way when her relative Mary visited her unexpectedly during her pregnancy. Rivalry was totally foreign to Elizabeth.[4]

Rather than talk about herself, she gave all her attention to Mary, whom she recognized at once as her superior. It became a meeting, not of an old woman and a young one, but of the mother of John—the preparer of the way—with the mother of Emmanuel, the Messiah, whose way must be prepared. That made a big difference. Elizabeth acknowledged this with a humility and modesty one could be envious of. She was not jealous in the least. She didn't find it difficult to call the much younger woman "the mother of my Lord" and "blessed among women."

4. I Corinthians 10:24

This was the work of the Holy Spirit in her. The ninefold fruits of the Spirit which Paul listed later[5] were already present in her. Even before Mary was able to share her great happiness. Elizabeth knew what was happening. Elizabeth saw—so to speak—the unborn Child and worshipped Him as her Lord. The other unborn child—the one in her—leapt with joy, as if he wanted to welcome his Master, the One he would humbly serve later on.[6]

At that moment, the woman who had been reproached for her childlessness became a prophetess. "Blessed is she that believes," she said, "for there shall be a performance of those things which were told her from the Lord."

For three months the mothers-to-be remained together— women who were writing history.

They talked a lot and laughed a lot, but uppermost in their minds was what God was going to do. Luke is very clear about this. It was no wonder that all the people in the hill country of Judea who lived near them, talked about John and his parents. People took what was happening to heart and said, "Watch that child. Wait and see what will become of him. God's hand is upon him in a special way."[7]

A new expectation broke loose. People began looking forward to what God was going to do. They were prepared for great things to come, for the Man who would come—Jesus, the Messiah. For all this God used Elizabeth, a woman of faith and remarkable character. What made her remarkable was that she was full of God.

God can use such a woman to accomplish marvelous things. Such a woman is a good life-partner.

Elizabeth, strong of character and a good life-partner (Luke 1:5-20, 24, 25, 39-45)

Questions:
1. What positive announcement does the Bible make about Elizabeth in Luke 1:6?

5. Galatians 5:22,23
6. John 3:30
7. Luke 1:65,66

2. What was the "reproach" of Elizabeth's life? Name other women in the Bible who had the same experience.
3. Consider Zacharias' song of praise (Luke 1:67-79) in the context of the story and describe how the couple's lack was amply compensated. (See also Matthew 11:11a.)
4. Study Elizabeth's life in light of Galatians 5:22,23. Which aspects of the fruit of the Spirit do you see in her life? (Also read Philippians 2:3,4 and I Corinthians 10:24.)
5. Are there indications that Elizabeth was a good wife? If so, what?
6. What appeals most to you in her life? In what way do you wish to follow her example? How will you do this?

17

*"Anna permitted her heartbreak to force her to God . . .
Those of us who have faced tragedy of any kind—
particularly those of you who are widows—know that
nothing heals the wounds like being consciously with God."*
Eugenia Price*

Anna,
a woman who wasn't destroyed
by a broken heart

Jeremiah 49:11 "Leave your orphans behind, I will keep them alive; and let your widows trust in Me."

Psalm 147:3 He heals the brokenhearted, and binds up their wounds.

Luke 2:22-27a And when the days for their purification according to the Law of Moses were completed, they brought Him up to Jerusalem to present Him to the Lord (as it is written in the Law of the Lord, "Every firstborn male that opens the womb shall be called holy to the Lord"), and to offer a sacrifice according to what was said in the Law of the Lord, "A pair of turtledoves, or two young pigeons." And behold, there was a man in Jerusalem whose name was Simeon; and this man was righteous and devout, looking for the consolation of Israel; and the Holy Spirit was upon him. And it had been revealed to him by the Holy Spirit that he would not see death before he had seen the Lord's Christ. And he came in the Spirit into the Temple.

Luke 2:36-38 And there was a prophetess, Anna the daughter of Phanuel, of the tribe of Asher. She was advanced in years, having

*Price, Eugenia. *The Unique World of Women,*
© 1969, Zondervan Publishing House, Grand Rapids, Michigan.

lived with a husband seven years after her marriage, and then as a widow to the age of eighty-four. And she never left the Temple, serving night and day with fastings and prayers. And at that very moment she came up and began giving thanks to God, and continued to speak of Him to all those who were looking for the redemption of Jerusalem.

Can a person die of a broken heart?

British medical doctors, studying the cases of a large group of widowers, discovered that a number of them died within the first six months after the deaths of their wives—50 percent of them through heart failure.

The prophetess Anna's life should have been without hope. Even today, a widow in the Middle East is practically thrown into the grave when her husband dies. The only thing a childless woman in Anna's time could do after the death of her husband was return to the house of her parents to wait for a second husband or death.

The happiness of Anna's marriage lasted only seven years. Bible commentators say that she had been a widow for over 60 years. She was a prophetess out of the tribe of Asher from Galilee. This was the insignificant tribe of which it had been said, "No prophets can come from Galilee."

Prophets were usually men. A female prophet was rare. The Bible names a few—Miriam, Deborah, Huldah and Noadiah in the Old Testament; and the four daughters of Philip the evangelist in the New Testament.

Anna stands between the Old and the New Testaments.

It was an honor to be a prophetess. A woman who, like a male prophet, spoke the Word of God to the people was exceptionally privileged. Anna belonged to a select group.

Widows often take the attitude, "When my husband died, my life stopped." Anna took a completely different point of view. She didn't flee to isolation and self-pity after the great blow in her life. She didn't become a burden to her relatives. She didn't become a lonely woman to whom life has nothing to offer, nor did she become a person whom everyone pitied, but no one knew how to help.

And she didn't flee into the past. This is one of the greatest dangers widows must face, and only those who, like Anna, have lost their life-partners know how serious this threat can be to their spiritual lives.

When the unity of a married couple is broken, what remains is a single person torn in two. Even after a relatively short marriage the one who remains behind is never the same personality he or she was before. He remains half of two people.

Was Anna comforted by the thought that God doesn't just take for the sake of taking away? Did she expect that He would give Himself in exchange for what He took from her? Most likely. A person must have courage and farsightedness to embrace that attitude. Jesus later told His disciples that no one who put his hand to the plow and looked back was fit for the Kingdom of God.[1]

Anna fled to God. She dedicated her life to serving Him in His Temple. She prayed and fasted. She was willing to give more attention to God than to herself and to give His work the highest priority.

When a widow dares to leave the past alone, when she is not dependent upon memories for true happiness, and when she dares to face both present and future with God, a supernatural peace floods her heart. She no longer stands in life as a bereft one, but as one who comforts. She can comfort others in problems and mourning because she herself has been comforted by God.[2]

Anna was occupied with God's work not only during the day, but also during the night. Yet despite all her activities, she didn't lose sight of people. A real walk with God isn't only introspective, it is outgoing. It wants to make others happy. Soren Kierkegaard once said, "The door of happiness opens to the outside . . . to others."

The world was dark, gloomy and without hope in Anna's day. The problems had become too great for the people to bear. Many, therefore, were looking consciously or subconsciously for a redemption which could only come from God—the coming of the Messiah.

Suddenly, the great day was there. Jesus was born!

When Joseph and Mary took their Firstborn to the Temple to present Him to God as required by the Law, they not only found

1. Luke 9:62
2. II Corinthians 1:3,4

the pious Simeon there, the man who knew he wouldn't die before seeing the Messiah, but they also saw Anna. God, who had cared for her so faithfully all these years, saw to it that she didn't miss that sacred moment. The woman who wouldn't have ordinarily had any chance in life because of her background, widowed status and age, at that moment became one of the most privileged women in the world. Together with Simeon she was allowed to see the Child and worship Him.

This was the crowning moment of her life, the answer to the prayers of many years. This was the greatest moment of all ages, the moment the world had been waiting for so anxiously—the Messiah had come!

It was only natural for Anna to do two things. First, she joined Simeon in praising and worshipping God because the long expected Redeemer of her people, of the world, and of her own sins, had come. Second, she decided she couldn't possibly keep this exciting news to herself. Someone has said, "Witnessing is taking a good look at the Lord Jesus Christ and then telling others what you have seen." This was Anna's response.

This proves how well she knew people. She knew all those in Jerusalem who were looking forward to the Saviour. She went and told these people what she had seen.

This proclaimer of Jesus Christ was not an energetic young man of eloquent speech, but an old woman. She was someone who had experienced what the psalmist had written about the Lord, "He heals the brokenhearted, and binds up their wounds."

Anna, a woman who wasn't destroyed by a broken heart
(Jeremiah 49:11; Psalm 147:3; Luke 2:22-27a, 36-38)

Questions:
1. As a young woman Anna experienced a great loss. How did this influence her life? (See also Luke 9:62.)

2. How does the Bible describe her relationship with God? What conclusions do you draw from this?
3. What privilege did Anna experience?
4. What did Anna do after she had seen Jesus?
5. Read II Corinthians 1:3,4. What specific opportunities do people who have encountered sorrow have?
6. What have you learned from Anna about how to have victory in sorrow? Is there someone you can help in this area? Who?

18

*"I will place no value on anything I may possess except
in relation to the Kingdom of Christ. If anything I have will
advance the interests of that Kingdom, it shall be
given away or kept, only as by giving or keeping it
I may promote the glory of Him, to whom I
owe all my hopes in time and eternity."* David Livingstone*

A widow
who knew how to handle money

Mark 12:41-44 And He sat down opposite the treasury, and began observing how the multitude were putting money into the treasury; and many rich people were putting in large sums. And a poor widow came and put in two small copper coins, which amount to a cent. And calling His disciples to Him, He said to them, "Truly I say to you, this poor widow put in more than all the contributors to the treasury; for they all put in out of their surplus, but she, out of her poverty, put in all she owned, all she had to live on."

II Corinthians 9:6-8 Now this I say, he who sows sparingly shall also reap sparingly; and he who sows bountifully shall also reap bountifully. Let each one do just as he has purposed in his heart; not grudgingly or under compulsion; for God loves a cheerful giver. And God is able to make all grace abound to you, that always having all sufficiency in everything, you may have an abundance for every good deed.

Jerusalem was busy that day. Jews from all over the known world were flocking to the city. It would soon be Passover and every devout Jew wanted to celebrate the festival days in the Holy City.

Studies in Christian Living, Book 6, "Growing in Service,"
© 1964, The Navigators, Colorado Springs, Colorado.

At home, the women were busily preparing the Passover meal. They had bought great quantities of food to cook and bake for the great feasts.

But one woman was not joining the festivities. She hadn't spent her money on foodstuffs because she didn't have much and, therefore, had to spend it wisely. She didn't earn much money— but she did know exactly what to do with what she had. She walked straight to the Temple and there, without any hesitation, she put her two tiny copper coins into the treasury box. Rich men jostled past her and threw great quantities of money into the box— money from their abundance. Then she withdrew as inconspicuously as she came.

Inconspicuously?

Not as far as Jesus was concerned. He was in the Temple. His visits to His Father's house were numbered. In a few more days He would be taken captive in a garden opposite the Temple Square, just across the Kidron Brook. He would then be crucified. Important things were about to happen. In fact, the most significant act of history was about to occur. Yet He had time to notice a poor widow give God her two pennies.

He stood watching people toss money into the treasury box. He saw the rich give a lot, and that was good. But their gifts hardly made a dent in their abundant possessions. They had so much left over. Then the poor widow had come. Jesus knew what she was doing. He knew that the two pennies were the last ones she possessed. She had literally given her entire worldly wealth to the God she loved. The pennies wouldn't reach far in paying the bills of the Temple—what could one buy for two pennies?

But Jesus thought her gift was so important that He drew His disciples' attention to it. He said, "This poor widow put more into the offering box than all the others. For while the others put in what they had to spare of their riches; she, poor as she is, put in all she had." To the Lord, how much she gave was not as important as how much she had left after giving. She had nothing left. Jesus was concerned with what the money represented to the giver. To this woman it represented everything.

Money itself has no value to God. Paul wrote, "The God who made the world and everything in it, being Lord of heaven and earth, does not live in shrines made by man, nor is He served by human hands, as though He needed anything, since He Himself gives to all men life and breath and everything."[1] God is interested in the motives of the person who gives. He knows that, by nature, people tend to hold their money closely. They often forget that only by God's grace can they earn money, since He gives health and a sound mind.[2] They often mistakenly think, "I can do what I like with my money."

God does not desire for people to give because He needs it. He only wants them to use their money in the right way. He knows that if a person gives of his substance to God he does so because he loves Him; because he wants to share all—even his possessions—with Him. Then He multiplies the actual value of the money, as He multiplied the loaves and the fish.[3] He can perform miracles with it. A person sharing all with God will discover that much can be done with little when God adds His blessing.

It is remarkable that this poor widow sensed the atmosphere of New Testament giving while she still lived under the Old Testament covenant where giving was governed by law, with God giving precise rules for spending money—ten percent of all income for His purposes.[4] From this ten percent the Temple servants, the Levites, were paid. No Jew could escape this obligation. Even the Levites had to, in turn, give ten percent of their money.[5]

But in the New Testament the situation was different. There were no stiff regulations, no set amounts. The motivating factor was love instead of law. And love cannot be regulated by law. It has to be a voluntary expression. Those who are guided by this principle have pleasure in giving. They give regularly.[6] They give unobtrusively.[7]

Did this woman sense that God was about to give His Son to the world? The greatest single act of love? Was this the reason she wanted to prove her love to Him by her total dedication? She understood that giving was not the exclusive privilege of the rich. Poor people have the same opportunity. The percentage that the poor can give of their wages is no smaller than the percentage the rich can give. While the actual amount may be smaller, the percentage remains the same.

Money does not need to be considered "vulgar." It has exciting

1. Acts 17:24,25　　　　4. Leviticus 27:30,32
2. Proverbs 10:22　　　　5. Numbers 18:21, 25-30
3. Luke 9:12-17　　　　　6. I Corinthians 16:2　　　　7. Matthew 6:2-4

potential when dedicated to God and His service. Then it has lasting value. "Money," someone once said, "is something you cannot take with you to heaven, but you can send it on ahead." It can be used for transactions of eternal value, as the widow's was. Money then becomes a capital investment in heaven.[8]

It is a pity that the veil covering this woman's life was lifted only slightly. It would be interesting to know how He, who was touched by her sacrificial gift, took care of her. Didn't He say through Solomon, "Honor the Lord from your wealth, and from the first of all your produce; so your barns will be filled with plenty, and your vats will overflow with new wine."[9] And through the mouth of Malachi hadn't He promised showerings of blessings to the person who gave just ten percent of his income?[10] The poor widow had not been satisfied to give only a part of her money. Ten percent was too small an act of devotion to God. She wanted to give one hundred percent. Since God doesn't want to be any man's debtor, there are no limitations to the blessings He could have bestowed upon this poor woman.

One thing is certain—she celebrated a wonderful Passover.

A widow who knew how to handle money
(Mark 12:41-44; II Corinthians 9:6-8)

Questions:
1. What was remarkable about the amount of money the widow contributed?
2. How did Jesus value this small amount (less than one cent) in view of other larger gifts?
3. What did God say about giving in the Old Testament? (Proverbs 3:9,10; Malachi 3:10)
4. What guidelines are given in the New Testament regarding giving? (II Corinthians 9:6,7; I Corinthians 16:2; Matthew 6:2-4)
5. How does God reward those who give their money to Him?
6. Did the widow's story influence you in the way you handle finances? If so, how?

---

8. Philippians 4:17   9. Proverbs 3:9,10   10. Malachi 3:10

19

*"My prayer for you is that you may have still more love—
a love that is full of knowledge and every wise
insight. I want you to be able always to recognize
the highest and the best."* Paul*

Martha of Bethany,
a woman who gave priority to secondary matters

Luke 10:38-42 Now as they were traveling along, He entered a
certain village; and a woman named Martha welcomed Him into her
home. And she had a sister called Mary, who moreover was
listening to the Lord's word, seated at His feet. But Martha was
distracted with all her preparations; and she came up to Him, and
said, "Lord, do Yóu not care that my sister has left me to do all the
serving alone? Then tell her to help me." But the Lord answered
and said to her, "Martha, Martha, you are worried and bothered
about so many things; but only a few things are necessary, really
only one, for Mary has chosen the good part, which shall not be
taken away from her."

John 11:17-27 So when Jesus came, He found that he had already
been in the tomb four days. Now Bethany was near Jerusalem,
about two miles off; and many of the Jews had come to Martha and
Mary, to console them concerning their brother. Martha therefore,
when she heard that Jesus was coming, went to meet Him; but Mary
still sat in the house. Martha therefore said to Jesus, "Lord, if You
had been here, my brother would not have died. Even now I know
that whatever You ask of God, God will give You." Jesus said to her,
"Your brother shall rise again." Martha said to Him, "I know that he

*Philippians 1:9-10a. Phillips, J. B. *The New Testament in Modern
English,* © 1972, The Macmillan Company, New York, N.Y.

will rise again in the resurrection on the last day." Jesus said to her, "I am the resurrection and the life; he who believes in Me shall live even if he dies, and everyone who lives and believes in Me shall never die. Do you believe this?" She said to Him, "Yes, Lord; I have believed that You are the Christ, the Son of God, even He who comes into the world."

John 11:32-44 Therefore, when Mary came where Jesus was, she saw Him, and fell at His feet, saying to Him, "Lord, if You had been here, my brother would not have died." When Jesus therefore saw her weeping, and the Jews who came with her, also weeping, He was deeply moved in spirit, and was troubled, and said, "Where have you laid him?" They said to Him, "Lord, come and see." Jesus wept. And so the Jews were saying, "Behold how He loved him!" But some of them said, "Could not this man, who opened the eyes of him who was blind, have kept this man also from dying?"
Jesus therefore again being deeply moved within, came to the tomb. Now it was a cave, and a stone was lying against it. Jesus said, "Remove the stone." Martha, the sister of the deceased, said to Him, "Lord, by this time there will be a stench; for he has been dead four days." Jesus said to her, "Did I not say to you, if you believe, you will see the glory of God?" And so they removed the stone. And Jesus raised His eyes, and said, "Father, I thank Thee that Thou heardest Me. And I knew that Thou hearest Me always; but because of the people standing around I said it, that they may believe that Thou didst send Me." And when He had said these things, He cried out with a loud voice, "Lazarus, come forth." He who had died came forth, bound hand and foot with wrappings; and his face was wrapped around with a cloth. Jesus said to them, "Unbind him, and let him go."

Martha was tense. A moment ago 13 guests, all men, had dropped in unexpectedly. They were Jesus, the Master, and His disciples, who were on their way to Jerusalem just two miles down the road.
The visitors were not unknown guests. Jesus was a good friend of Martha, her sister Mary and their brother Lazarus. He sometimes arrived with His disciples late at night to stay with them in Bethany.

Martha was grateful that the Master, who had no place to lay His head,[1] felt at home with them. She was hospitable and lovingly opened her home to others. She considered it an honor to please her guests.

She wrestled with herself as she attended to the needs of the dusty and hungry men. It was not that her home was not spacious enough or that her pantry was poorly provided with food. She was rich enough. However, she was irritated because her sister, Mary, was not helping her serve.

Mary was totally absorbed as she listened to the Master. She eagerly drank in His every word. The uppermost question in her mind was "How can I enjoy Him the most? What can I learn?"

Martha was no less happy to have Jesus visit them than her sister, but she did not enjoy it as completely. Her thoughts were constantly occupied by details and secondary issues. That was why the greatness of the occasion escaped her. She was nervous. Irritated! And, as usual in such a situation, she found fault with the other person.

Martha suffered from self-pity. "Lord," she interrupted, "Don't You care that my sister has left me to serve alone?"

Martha didn't seem to care that she was accusing her sister in the presence of her guests and that she was implicating Jesus in the accusation! And that was not all. She dared to order the Master to make Mary come and help her.

The voice of the Master, which had kept the listeners spellbound, stopped abruptly. "Martha, Martha," He said, "You worry and trouble yourself over so many things, but only one is necessary. Mary has chosen the right thing, and it should not be taken away from her."

With those few words He implied much more. They contained a warning: *Martha, how can you mingle the primary and secondary issues in such a manner? How can you become lost in things of minor importance while I am in your home? Martha, don't you understand that I came in the first place to serve? Not to be served?[2] Don't you see that I am much more interested in you than in shelter and food? I do appreciate your hospitality, but My first concern is for Martha, not the hostess. Martha, you are so efficient and wise—why must you do everything, even the smallest detail,*

1. Matthew 8:20
2. Matthew 20:28

by yourself? Don't you understand that I prefer a simple meal anyway? In My Kingdom priority is given to spiritual matters. Examine yourself. Know your own heart. Look at things from My point of view.

Mary, He continued, *doesn't need to receive correction; you do. But I say all this only because I love you.*[3] *Things of temporal value, worries about this life choke My Word*[4] *and darken your view of eternal matters. Also, Martha, be careful about judging someone else.*[5] *Leave that to Me instead.*[6] *Test yourself and judge your own heart.*[7]

The next meeting between Jesus and this family took place under extremely sad circumstances. Sickness and fear had entered the happy home. Lazarus was seriously ill. Without delay his sisters had sent a message to Jesus, who was preaching on the other side of the Jordan River. All they said to Him was, "Lord, Your friend is very ill."

They had expected Him to come right away. They knew when it would be possible for Him to come there. But Jesus stayed away—on purpose—and Lazarus died.

God would be glorified through this illness in a special way. Mary and Martha would not rejoice about their brother's healing, but about his resurrection from the dead.

This was beyond their perception. Therefore, the sisters repeated many times a day, "If the Lord had been here Lazarus would not have died."

Then, when Lazarus had been buried for four days and the house was full of comforting friends, Jesus arrived. Mary, overcome by sorrow, stayed at home, but Martha's character could not deny itself. How could she sit quietly at home when the Master was coming? Impossible! She went to meet Him and repeated what she and Mary had said so often, "This would not have happened, Lord, if You had been here."

Again, there was a tinge of accusation in her words to Jesus, but they were also an expression of faith and hope. She proved this when she added, "But I know that even now God will give You whatever You ask of Him."

All was not lost.

3. Hebrews 12:5,6
4. Mark 4:19   6. I Corinthians 4:5
5. Matthew 7:1,2   7. II Corinthians 13:5

When He promised, "Your brother will be raised to life," Martha thought of the distant future. But Jesus confronted her with an overwhelming fact, "I am the resurrection and the life."

The resurrection didn't offer hope for the future only. It was a present reality. That reality was personified in the Man who was speaking to her. He not only gave life, He was life Himself.

Martha's answer was a remarkable confession of faith, "Yes, Lord! I do believe that You are the Messiah, the Son of God, who has come into the world."

The question that so many had asked and that had brought such division was: "Is He the Christ or not?"[8] Martha had given a positive answer even though she could not imagine the implication of her testimony.

What happened next is very moving. Martha had called Mary. She arrived and greeted Jesus. They saw that Jesus was deeply sorrowful. The words of Isaiah became reality, "In all their affliction He was afflicted."[9]

The Son of God was not ashamed of His tears. He wept.

The sisters and all who had come to mourn saw it. Some said, "See how much He loved him." Others were critical saying, "He opened the blind man's eyes, didn't He? Then why couldn't He keep Lazarus from dying?"

Then Jesus' sufferings came to light. He would not only suffer in His own approaching death. In this holy moment, when He proved His victory over death, Jesus suffered in life. He had done that every day of His earthly existence. He had suffered from the misunderstanding of the people.[10] He had suffered from the unfaithfulness of His friends.[11] He also suffered because of Martha—in the way she used her energy—in the way she interfered.

Again she interrupted Him. When He gave the order to remove the stone from the grave, she thought it necessary to remind Him that Lazarus, having been in the grave for four days, would be in a state of decomposition.

"Didn't I tell you that you would see God's glory if you believed?" Jesus answered.

Upon His shout, "Lazarus, come out!" death released its prey. Lazarus stood before them, alive. They could touch him. Jesus,

8. John 7:31, 41-43; Matthew 11:3   10. Mark 6:1-6
9. Isaiah 63:9   11. Luke 22:39-45; Matthew 26:31-35

who had taken upon Himself the blame of insensitivity to the sorrow of His friends, now sealed His friendship with the people of Bethany with His life.

Now His freedom was limited. He needed to hide Himself in order not to fall into the hands of the Pharisees and chief priests prematurely.[12] In a few weeks He would die on the Cross. He would die not only for the sins of Lazarus, Martha and Mary, but also for the sins of the whole world.

Six days before Jesus' death, Martha served at a banquet given in His honor.[13] The story is told in few words. Martha had not stopped serving. She had not fallen from one extreme to another. She was a woman of striking character. The beautiful characteristics of hospitality and a willingness to serve were still evident. She was also a woman whose faith, by the death of Lazarus, had stood the test.

She was also a courageous woman. She remained faithful to the Lord at a time when the hatred of the Jews was the most vehement and would result in His death.

Jesus loved her. He extended to her the honor of His friendship.

He, who knew people, understood that women like Martha can suffer needlessly simply because of themselves. He knew that a good, intelligent, energetic woman like her could easily stumble because of too much drive, because of a desire to interfere. She must be particularly careful not to get lost in matters of secondary importance. Women like Martha have a particular need for Jesus. He can keep them from dedicating their lives to the second best.

Martha of Bethany, a woman who gave priority to secondary matters
(Luke 10:38-42; John 11:17-27, 32- 44. Also see the Bible passages under Mary of Bethany in the following chapter.)

Questions:
1. What characterized the family in Bethany?

---

12. John 11:53,54
13. John 12:1,2

2. What do you consider to be Martha's major positive characteristic? (Read also Mark 11:11 and Matthew 21:17.)
3. Do you see dangers connected with this characteristic in her life? If so, what are they?
4. What facts lead to the conclusion that Martha did indeed give priority to issues of secondary importance?
5. Read John 11. What does this chapter teach about Martha's faith?
6. In what way is Martha an example or warning to you? How are you going to apply what you have learned from her?

20

"Friendship with God is reserved for those who reverence Him. With them alone He shares the secrets of His promises." David*

Mary of Bethany, a woman with insight to choose the best

John 12:1-11 Jesus, therefore, six days before the Passover, came to Bethany where Lazarus was, whom Jesus had raised from the dead. So they made Him a supper there; and Martha was serving; but Lazarus was one of those reclining at the table with Him. Mary therefore took a pound of very costly, genuine spikenard ointment, and anointed the feet of Jesus, and wiped His feet with her hair; and the house was filled with the fragrance of the ointment. But Judas Iscariot, one of His disciples, who was intending to betray Him, said, "Why was this ointment not sold for three hundred denarii, and given to poor people?" Now he said this, not because he was concerned about the poor, but because he was a thief, and as he had the money box, he used to pilfer what was put into it. Jesus therefore said, "Let her alone, in order that she may keep it for the day of My burial. For the poor you always have with you; but you do not always have Me."

The great multitude therefore of the Jews learned that He was there; and they came, not for Jesus' sake only, but that they might also see Lazarus, whom He raised from the dead. But the chief priests took counsel that they might put Lazarus to death also; because on account of him many of the Jews were going away, and were believing in Jesus.

*Psalm 25:14. Taylor, Kenneth N. *The Living Bible,*
© 1971, Tyndale House Publishers, Wheaton, Illinois.

Matthew 26:13 "Truly I say to you, wherever this gospel is preached in the whole world, what this woman has done shall also be spoken of in memory of her."

She was hardly noticed when she entered the room. She glanced at the men there and then seated herself behind the guest of honor. With a simple motion she arranged her long dress and felt for the little jar still hidden between its pleats. Wonderful—the conversation of the guests had not been disturbed by her entrance. The deep voices of the men continued to fill the room as before. She was accustomed to sitting at the feet of Jesus, and those present had seen her do this before.[1]

While the men ate and talked, Mary's thoughts went back to the first time that Jesus and His disciples had come to her home. He had also entered her life and—as He alone could do—had brought about a radical change. She didn't recognize her own life anymore. "He started by giving us His friendship," she mused. That was an unknown experience. Up until that time a wide gulf had existed between men and women. After all, didn't the Jewish men thank God every morning in their prayers that He had created them "not as a slave, nor a heathen nor a woman"?

It had been apparent immediately that He was different. His concern was not just for a man or just for a woman. He was interested in the total human being, man or woman.[2]

He had introduced a new respect for women. He had offered her possibilities that had been unknown until then. He had lifted her to His plan. That was why she had felt so entirely at ease in His presence. Without any shyness, she had come and sat down in the midst of the men who were listening to His words.

Sitting at His feet and listening to Him, there was a hunger in her heart, a thirst after God. The purpose of her existence had become clear in listening to this man. A conviction grew within her, "I am created for God. I exist because of Him."[3]

This gave meaning and color to her life. It revealed previously undreamed of opportunities. She lived her life in the fellowship of Christ.[4] This was the purpose of life to which she felt called. The first result was a hunger for His Word. Bread—food for the body

1. Luke 10:39   3. Revelation 4:11
2. Galatians 3:28   4. I Corinthians 1:9

alone—could not satisfy a human being. The inner person must be fed with the Word of God.[5]

While she satisfied her thirst with His words and her knowledge about Him increased, her feelings matured into a decision, "I shall do for Him what I can." Gratitude swelled in her heart. She watched the men talking for a moment longer. Then she was distracted by Martha, who waited upon the Lord and the other men. *Martha,* she thought, *how much He has done for you! So very much.* Martha had an active, outgoing personality. Her love for the Lord revealed itself in her service for Him because she was a woman who thought and acted quickly. She was the opposite of Mary, who was more introspective and quiet by nature. It was encouraging to see how the Lord understood both of them. He loved each one according to her own character.

From Martha, Mary's eyes wandered to Lazarus, the host, who was sitting next to the Master. She could not help feasting her eyes upon her brother. He had come back from the dead. He lived! Until she died she would never forget the moment when Jesus had raised His voice and shouted, "Lazarus, come out!"

There was also some shame in her heart when she remembered that occasion. Martha and she had wondered why the Master hadn't come more quickly. They could not understand His delay which had been almost more painful than the loss of their brother. Never before in their lives had they felt so deserted. Looking back they could see how shortsighted they had been. Later, they had understood why Christ had acted this way. He had done it entirely for His Father's will, for Lazarus' resurrection had honored God. Many people were moved to believe.

To honor God and provide salvation for His people—that was Jesus' aim. This proved to be hard for Jesus, for the fiery hatred of the Jewish leaders, which had only been smouldering to this point, now was stirred up into a flame which would destroy Him. While snatching Lazarus away from death, He had signed His own death sentence.

In six days it would be Passover.

Did this thought suddenly open her eyes? Did she feel instinctively that Jesus had come today to say farewell? He was also preparing for the festivities at hand. This Passover there would not only be blood shed at the Temple from the animals sacrificed to redeem the sins of the people,[6] but in Jerusalem a greater sacrifice would be offered. Jesus would die.

She remembered all the times He had spoken of His sufferings to come.[7] She realized that the hatred of many Jewish leaders had reached its boiling point. There remained no question in her mind: Jesus would have to die. He was the Lamb of God who would take away the sin not of a single nation, but of the entire world.[8]

Much had become clear to Mary during her friendship with Jesus as she saturated herself with His words. She had developed a spiritual insight and understanding of things which other people didn't see.

In the Word of God, faith and deeds inseparably belong together. Mary felt this in the depths of her soul. She felt a stirring desire to do something. She wanted to express her thankfulness to her Lord, perhaps for the last time. Her hands moved along her robe. They touched the little jar hidden there. Her decision was made.

The perfume was very costly. The amount in the jar represented a laborer's wages for an entire year.[9] Nard was an embalming oil. *This belongs at a funeral,* she thought. *No!* She suppressed this thought as quickly as it came to her mind. It was the living Lord who must receive her worship, not the dead. It was time to do something for Him now.

She quickly carried out her plan as if she were afraid someone would keep her from doing it—as if there were not much time left—

The sweet smelling drops of perfume pouring out upon Jesus' feet, were an expression of Mary's gratitude. Without holding back, she poured out her soul. Her homage was without words. How could simple words express her many thoughts? Sometimes it is easier to convey one's deepest thoughts by a look or motion rather than words.

Her surroundings were completely forgotten, as she was taken up with her thoughts about the Lord. Lovingly she dried His feet with her hair. Suddenly the room was silent. The talking had stopped. The thick perfumed odor had pervaded the room—it filled the entire house. Mary, who had wanted to honor the Lord

---

6. Exodus 12:13, 21-28   8. John 1:29
7. Mark 8:31   9. Matthew 20:2

unnoticed, had, by the spreading smell, placed herself squarely in the center of attention. What had she done?

What to the Master was a sweet smell was offensive to the nostrils of Judas Iscariot. His criticism was biting, "Why wasn't this perfume sold for three hundred dollars, and the money given to the poor?" Others supported him. Although Judas sounded altruistic, his interest in the poor was a pretense. He would rather have put the cash in the money bag he carried so that he could help himself.

Again Mary's good intentions were interpreted the wrong way, like the time she had been accused of laziness by her sister.[10] Jesus knew her motives, however. He had also defended her on that occasion. Now He said, "Leave her alone! Why are you bothering her? She has done a fine and beautiful thing for Me."[11]

Mary was the only one who realized His time on earth was drawing to an end. Anything she could do for Him was more important than anything else.

He not only defended her, but He praised her, "She did what she could."[12]

Quietly listening to His words had helped Mary grow into a woman with spiritual insight. She had become a woman who understood the secrets of God. She knew precisely what to do and when.

The Master's words not only revealed Mary's thoughts—they also clarified the way God looked at things. His highest praise was reserved for the person who was interested in His Word and who acted upon it. Such a person didn't need to fear criticism from his fellow men. He didn't need to withdraw when they nagged at him. Such a person had the best advocate available—Jesus Himself.

Again Mary was not rebuked. On the contrary, right then Jesus erected a monument for her that would stand through the ages. It was better than any monument of stone or bronze. "Now, remember this! Wherever the Gospel is preached, what she has done will be told about her."[13]

The smell of Mary's perfume has permeated the entire world— even to this day. Thousands, no, millions have praised her. They have been stimulated by her, because she did what she could. Mary was a woman with insight who chose the best.

10. Luke 10:40,41   12. Mark 14:8
11. Mark 14:6   13. Mark 14:9

Mary of Bethany, a woman with insight to choose the best
(John 12:1-11; Matthew 26:13. Also see Bible passages under
Martha in the previous chapter.)

Questions:
1. What is the first striking characteristic of Mary revealed in Luke
   10:38- 42?
2. What was Jesus' appraisal of her?
3. Consider Mary's life in the light of Matthew 4:4 and I Corinthians 1:9 and list your findings.
4. What thoughts do you have after reading about Mary in John
   12:1-8? (Read also Matthew 26:6-13 and Mark 14:3-9.)
5. List the things that Jesus said of Mary. Which of these impresses
   you the most? Why?
6. Which aspects of her life should you give more attention to in
   your own life? What are you going to do about it?

*"Christ led me to the experience of the overwhelming reality . . .
what this means in a life of unknown liberation, perspective,
joy and general change, cannot be told in words."*
Wilhelmina, former Queen of the Netherlands*

The Samaritan,
a woman who said yes to Jesus

John 4:4-26 And He had to pass through Samaria. So He came to a
city of Samaria, called Sychar, near the parcel of ground that Jacob
gave to his son Joseph; and Jacob's well was there. Jesus
therefore, being wearied from His journey, was sitting thus by the
well. It was about the sixth hour. There came a woman of Samaria
to draw water. Jesus said to her, "Give Me a drink." For His disciples
had gone away into the city to buy food. The Samaritan woman
therefore said to Him, "How is it that You, being a Jew, ask me for a
drink since I am a Samaritan woman?" (For Jews have no dealings
with Samaritans.) Jesus answered and said to her, "If you knew the
gift of God, and who it is who says to you, 'Give Me a drink,' you
would have asked Him, and He would have given you living water."
She said to Him, "Sir, You have nothing to draw with and the well is
deep; where then do You get that living water? You are not greater
than our father Jacob, are You, who gave us the well, and drank of it
himself, and his sons, and his cattle?" Jesus answered and said to
her, "Everyone who drinks of this water shall thirst again; but
whoever drinks of the water that I shall give him shall never thirst;
but the water that I shall give him shall become in him a well of
water springing up to eternal life." The woman said to Him, "Sir,
give me this water, so I will not be thirsty, nor come all the way here

*Wilhelmina. *Lonely, But Not Alone,*
translated from the Dutch by John Peereboom,
© 1960, McGraw-Hill Inc., New York, N.Y.

to draw." He said to her, "Go, call your husband, and come here." The woman answered and said, "I have no husband." Jesus said to her, "You have well said, 'I have no husband'; for you have had five husbands; and the one whom you now have is not your husband; this you have said truly." The woman said to Him, "Sir, I perceive that You are a prophet. Our fathers worshipped in this mountain; and you people say that in Jerusalem is the place where men ought to worship." Jesus said to her, "Woman, believe Me, an hour is coming when neither in this mountain, nor in Jerusalem, shall you worship the Father. You worship that which you do not know; we worship that which we know; for salvation is from the Jews. But an hour is coming, and now is, when the true worshippers shall worship the Father in spirit and truth; for such people the Father seeks to be His worshippers. God is spirit; and those who worship Him must worship in spirit and truth." The woman said to Him, "I know that Messiah is coming (He who is called Christ); when that One comes, He will declare all things to us." Jesus said to her, "I who speak to you am He."

John 4:39-42 And from that city many of the Samaritans believed in Him because of the word of the woman who testified, "He told me all the things that I have done." So when the Samaritans came to Him, they were asking Him to stay with them; and He stayed there two days. And many more believed because of His word; and they were saying to the woman, "It is no longer because of what you said that we believe, for we have heard for ourselves and know that this One is indeed the Saviour of the world."

Reluctantly, she lifted the empty water pitcher up to her shoulder and, under the scorching noonday sun, set out along the dusty road from Sychar. She hated the very idea of this journey, but she had no alternative. She was too poor to pay a servant and being a woman of bad reputation, she didn't dare go to the well at a later hour when the air would be cooler. She could not run the risk of meeting the other villagers when they went to the well to draw their daily ration of water.

She had given up her feminine purity for immorality, and she paid for it daily. She was an outcast without friends. This was a consequence of the kind of life she was leading. And in a small village it was especially noticeable.

While still a long way away, she saw a Man sitting by the well. Even from that distance she could see that He was weary. As she approached, she saw by His dress and features that He was a Jew. She wondered what had brought this Man to this place. Jews had such a deep-rooted hatred of their brother-people, the Samaritans, that they avoided Samaria at all costs. When traveling from Judea to Galilee, they usually made a wide detour around the country. "Samaritans," they would say, "have no part in life after death." And, "He who eats the bread of a Samaritan is like someone who eats pork." Nothing could be more contemptible.

Her amazement increased when the Man asked her a favor. He was unlike any other Man—could it be His voice? He spoke with authority, but was not dictatorial. Or was it His expression, His human interest?

She was uncomfortable, ill at ease in the presence of His forceful personality. It is understandable that she could not place Him as the Master, for not only did the Jews have nothing whatsoever to do with the Samaritans, it was even forbidden for a Jewish man to talk to a woman on the street. "It would be better that the Articles of the Law be burned than that their contents be revealed to a woman publicly," said their rabbis.

Why then did this Man seek to contact her—not only a Samaritan, but a woman as well?

Jesus disregarded her question. He aroused her curiosity by speaking about living water. If she only knew who it was that was talking to her—the words "living water" struck her. That would be the answer to her problem. That would mean no more daily, dreaded journeys to draw water. She didn't realize that the water of all the world's oceans could not quench her thirst. A solution to her material problem was not the real answer. Her deepest need was in her soul.

And that was just where Jesus was aiming. He wanted to make her conscious of the necessity of meeting this need. He had come to Samaria for this purpose.

She didn't understand Him. Engrossed as she was in her daily problems, she had neglected the needs of her soul. "Give me some of this water so that I will not be thirsty again," she said. "Then," she continued, "I will not need to come to this well every day."

His answer was a simple, but most bewildering request, "Go, call your husband and then come back."

Your husband, your husband—but she had no lawful husband. It was frightening when this Man spoke these words, especially when the conversation had been progressing so favorably. She had had a lot of experience as far as men were concerned, but she could not lie to this One. "I don't have a husband," she retorted. "I am not married."

"That is correct. You have had five men and you are not married to the man with whom you are now living."

This was dreadful. Were there no secrets from this Man? Her life was like an open book to Him.[1] And yet, He neither despised nor blamed her. How strange! He had, however, made her conscious of the sick spot in her life—sin. Furthermore, He proved that He could not give her the coveted living water until this sin had been removed. As a religious woman she was fully aware of the laws concerning adultery. So far, however, she had been able to justify her actions by excuses.

But that time was past. She now clearly saw that her life had been governed by sin. Sin which could not continue in the eyes of God. Sin which had to be condemned—forcefully.

"I see that You are a Prophet, Sir," was all she could say. Then she began to talk about religion—how its forms and controversies divided the people. Religion always proved to be an interesting topic, and very safe. One could spend endless hours in discussions, making long arguments in which one could completely hide his true feelings.

Jesus stuck to the main subject of the conversation. He was not to be diverted from the purpose for which He had come. He showed her with a few words that religion was not a matter of form, but of content. God was looking for people who would seek Him with all their hearts, who would want to serve Him totally. The only thing valuable in God's sight was faith. This was what He was telling her. He didn't speak with a stately "truly, truly, I say . . . " as He had to the learned Nicodemus,[2] but simply asked, "Woman, believe Me." The desired result was the same—a new birth.

1. Hebrews 4:13
2. John 3:5

A longing for the Messiah filled her heart. The Christ—He would clarify everything which was still dark and obscure. Right then the conversation reached its climax. Jesus assured her that her longing was fulfilled, the future could become the present, then and there.

"I am the Messiah." Christ was not a figure in the distant future. He was flesh and blood. He stood before her. What He had told no one else so plainly, He disclosed to her, "I am the Christ."

For her, only for her, He had come to the much hated Samaria. For her He had bypassed Jewish rules and regulations. The messianic hour had come. Time for discrimination was past. There was a solution for racial hatred and religious controversy. Every human being, even the most sinful, could now come to God through Him on two conditions:

First, he must acknowledge his sin[3] and confess it.[4] He must acknowledge that he cannot exist before a righteous God, for He is holy. Second, he must rely on Jesus Christ—that is, believe in Him. He is the Mediator between God and man.[5] He bridged the gap which sin had made between man and God.

In a split second she saw it all very clearly. She was sinful, horrible, contemptible. He was full of love and understanding— forgiving. She understood that this was the reason He sought her. She received Him into her heart. She said yes to Jesus Christ.

Queen Wilhelmina of the Netherlands, another woman who said yes to Christ, wrote an impressive autobiography at the close of her life entitled *Lonely, But Not Alone*. She ended this book with what she calls the revelation of her life—that Christ wants to enter the human heart and govern it. Her last words are from the Bible, "Behold, I stand at the door and knock; if any one hears My voice and opens the door, I will come in to him and eat with him, and he with Me."[6]

Queen Wilhelmina considered herself to be a child of God and rightly so, for she had received Christ as her Saviour and Lord.[7] Anyone who receives Christ in such a manner becomes a new creation.[8] There is a vast difference between the backgrounds of the Samaritan woman and this queen. Yet their deepest experiences were the same, since receiving Jesus Christ as Saviour is the most important experience in any human life.

3. Romans 3:23   5. John 14:6   7. John 1:12
4. Romans 10:9,10   6. Revelation 3:20   8. II Corinthians 5:17

The woman with a broken, battered past was inwardly free. Free from the penalty of sin and, therefore, in God's sight, free from the stain of the past. People's criticism would no longer need to hurt her. From now on she could look people freely in the eye—unashamed. He who judged people, not by their outward appearance but according to their heart, had declared her free. How then could people accuse her?

The solution to her problems was total—both spiritual and material. The source of living water had cleansed her, quenched her thirst, and brought her a happiness she had never thought possible.

She was certainly not going to keep this to herself. She forgot why she had come to the well. There was something more important at stake. She hurried back to the village to spread the wonderful news that the Messiah had come. Sin could be forgiven. She must tell the people this—immediately!

She spoke to the people with the simple directness and freedom of one who has been in the presence of God, telling them of her experience.

"Come with me," she begged, "and meet the Man who knew my whole past. He surely must be the Christ."

Her shyness was gone. She spoke about her disreputable past without hesitation or fear. It was remarkable that this past life, of which she had been so ashamed, should become the link with the happy present.

The people, seeing the change in her, hurried from the village to Jacob's well. There they met the Messiah. Jesus did for them what He had done for the woman. He set them free. He gave them new life—eternal life.

They were impressed and begged Him to stay longer. So He did. Even more people came to listen to Him, and more—and more.

They told the woman, "We believe not because of what you have said, but because we have heard Him ourselves. We are personally convinced that He is the Saviour of the world." And that was good. Christ should have the attention, not the woman. Christ should get the glory. She was only a finger pointing toward Him.

Four years passed.[9] The earth and the heavens had been covered with a thick darkness on the day when the innocent Jesus of

Nazareth, both God and Man, was crucified.

After the crucifixion, the angels proclaimed His resurrection—and forty days later at His ascension they proclaimed His return to earth. Some days later the Holy Spirit descended from heaven. First on individuals, then on large crowds. Thousands and thousands of people experienced the beginning of a new life.

Then the awful persecution of the new believers arrived. Satan didn't—and doesn't—release his prey easily. When it became too dangerous for the Christians to remain in Jerusalem, they fled to Judea and Samaria.

A great evangelistic movement began in Samaria. It was so successful that an evangelist was needed to further the ministry. When Philip came and preached to great crowds, many turned to Christ. Again there was happiness in the town, culminating in the outpouring of the Holy Spirit. Differences between Jews and Samaritans were abolished forever. The Gospel was poured out upon the world. The Good News was spreading from town to town. And because of her willingness to share, the evangelistic movement in Samaria will forever be associated with a woman.

The story of the Samaritan woman plainly illustrates how although a person without Christ is a mission field, at the moment of receiving Him, this same person becomes a missionary—a missionary for Him by His grace. The entering of God's Son into a person's life makes the big difference.

The Samaritan, a woman who said yes to Jesus
(John 4:4-26, 39-42)

Questions:
1. Why do you think the Samaritan woman did not fetch water at a later, cooler hour? (The sixth hour is 12:00 noon.)
2. Why do you think Jesus told her to "Go, call your husband and come here"?

3. The woman talked about secondary religious issues. What was the real issue Jesus tried to point out to her? (Read Romans 3:23; 10:9-11.)
4. Consider this story in light of John 1:12 and Revelation 3:20. What are your conclusions?
5. Compare John 4:39-42 with II Corinthians 5:17 and list your findings.
6. What do you think were the two greatest results of this woman's talk with Jesus? (Check also Acts 8:1-17.)
7. What is there in this story regarding believing in Christ and witnessing for Him that has personally stimulated you? What practical action will you take in your life as a result of this?

"When a young woman really accepts her not being married, then this means such a liberation to her that in her unmarried situation she can make her special feminine characteristics useful to the most."
Dr. Paul Tournier*

Dorcas,
a woman who loved God

Acts 9:36-42 Now in Joppa there was a certain disciple named Tabitha (which translated in Greek is called Dorcas); this woman was abounding with deeds of kindness and charity, which she continually did. And it came about at that time that she fell sick and died; and when they had washed her body, they laid it in an upper room. And since Lydda was near Joppa, the disciples, having heard that Peter was there, sent two men to him, entreating him, "Do not delay to come to us." And Peter arose and went with them. And when he had come, they brought him into the upper room; and all the widows stood beside him weeping, and showing all the tunics and garments that Dorcas used to make while she was with them. But Peter sent them all out and knelt down and prayed, and turning to the body, he said, "Tabitha, arise." And she opened her eyes, and when she saw Peter, she sat up. And he gave her his hand and raised her up; and calling the saints and widows, he presented her alive. And it became known all over Joppa, and many believed in the Lord.

Romans 12:4-8 For just as we have many members in one body and all the members do not have the same function, so we, who are many, are one body in Christ, and individually members one of

*Tournier, Paul. *The Healing of Persons,*
© 1965, Harper & Row, Publishers, New York, N.Y.

another. And since we have gifts that differ according to the grace given to us, let each exercise them accordingly: if prophecy, according to the proportion of his faith; if service, in his serving; or he who teaches, in his teaching; or he who exhorts, in his exhortation; he who gives, with liberality; he who leads, with diligence; he who shows mercy, with cheerfulness.

James 1:27 This is pure and undefiled religion in the sight of our God and Father, to visit orphans and widows in their distress, and to keep oneself unstained by the world.

Dorcas was not a particularly striking woman. The only thing she did well was sewing, and who would call that remarkable? Many women could do as much.

Dorcas was a woman with one talent.[1] She had only one gift, and even that was an inconspicuous one. It would have been easy for Dorcas to think, *I am no prophetess like Miriam and I cannot rule a country like Deborah. I am not a woman who will play a large role in the history of my country. I don't belong in the category of gifted women.*

It seems that marriage and motherhood had also bypassed her. Otherwise, she could have indirectly influenced society through her husband or son. Wasn't it true that in the history of her country the destiny of a king of Israel had often been decided by his mother?

Yet there is one thing in which Dorcas surpassed every other woman in the Bible. She is the only one who was called a disciple! Dorcas was a disciple, a follower of Jesus, and that changed everything.

She opened her heart to Him before she followed Him. He became her Saviour before He became her Lord. And although she had received Him as her Redeemer she didn't stop there. Faith is more than just fellowship with God. One uses it to serve others— true faith expresses itself in deeds. A person who follows Christ is moved toward people as He was. He becomes creative and wants to do all he can to give his life maximum purpose. Therefore, the disciple Dorcas did what came naturally to her. She sewed, especially for the poor widows. She sewed to the best of her ability.

1. Matthew 25:14-29

Joppa (now Jaffa), a port along the Mediterranean Sea, must have had a large population of widows. During the season of bad weather, many of its fishermen were shipwrecked and drowned. These women had lost not only their husbands but their incomes. There was no Social Security in those days, but that really wasn't necessary, for, again and again, God had told His people to take good care of the widows and orphans.[2] If the people obeyed God's orders, then the widows had no needs and the people enjoyed abundant blessing, as the reward which God had promised them.[3]

God had promised that He would be their husband.[4] They enjoyed His special protection and care. Being a disciple, Dorcas knew what made her Lord happy, and that was to take care of this group of people in whom He was interested in a special way. Therefore, she didn't do her work halfheartedly. It wasn't just a pastime to her. She did it with a definite goal in mind. She did it with all her heart because she loved God. When Jesus had entered her heart, Dorcas had become a free woman. He had called Himself the Truth.[5] He stated further that those who were freed by Him are *truly* free.[6] Dorcas operated from this base of freedom.

The Bible leaves room for the thought that Dorcas was an unmarried woman, but this does not seem to have caused her to be frustrated by feelings of inferiority. She had no desire to compete in importance with the married women around her. She was not jealous of mothers with children.

Dorcas became a woman who was far ahead of her time. She experienced a fulfillment in life while working on her own, which was unique for the time in which she lived. Many women living in Jaffa today would certainly be glad to exchange places with her. Dorcas met a real need by sewing. She required little for herself. She lived for others.

A woman who is truly free is free to be herself and can develop her character in the way God uniquely created her. Someone who is free inside is a happy person who distributes happiness. Society cannot do without these people. Such a woman doesn't feel she has to fight for her rights. She doesn't have to work hard to become somebody—she already is somebody.

That was the reason for her own happiness. "He who wants to win happiness has to share it. Happiness was born as twins," Lord Byron, the English poet, later said.

Many of the widows in Joppa were walking around in clothing

2. Exodus 22:22-24; Deuteronomy 10:17,18

3. Deuteronomy 14:29; 24:19   5. John 14:6

4. Isaiah 54:4,5   6. John 8:32,36

sewn by Dorcas. There was a growing gratitude toward her. Dorcas, who probably stood alone in life, was most likely able to give moral and spiritual support to the widows. She understood lonely women and could talk with them. Consequently, she utilized her potential. In so doing, she became a person of importance in the church. Then came a sudden blow. Dorcas became ill and died.

Someone remembered that Peter was working in Lydda, only ten miles away and hastily sent two men to fetch him. They knew that he possessed supernatural power. Hadn't they heard that sick people were restored when Peter's shadow fell on them?[7] Hadn't he and John healed a lame man?[8] All their hopes were centered on him. Peter came right away. In the upper room where the dead body lay, Peter was encircled by weeping women. They told him how terribly they missed Dorcas, how bereft they were without her. They showed him the clothes she had made for them.

Often only good things are said of the dead. In this case, however, it was very obvious how those who stayed behind were suffering from the loss of the life which had been taken. Dorcas' love for them had given them a great love for her. What else could be expected? Peter did what he saw the Lord do in a similar situation.[9] He asked everyone to leave the room, then he prayed and restored Dorcas to life through the power of God.

The Bible records accounts of seven people who were raised from the dead. Dorcas was the only adult woman among them. The news of her resurrection became the talk of the day in Joppa. "Did you hear?" the people exclaimed to one another. "Dorcas is alive again! Peter has raised her from the dead."

Then something else remarkable occurred. The people realized that God had wrought a miracle, so they honored God Himself rather than Dorcas or Peter. Through these happenings people realized the emptiness of their own lives. They also desired to believe in the Lord Jesus. They began to understand some of the real values in life. They wanted to belong to Him as Dorcas did. They desired to become Christians, new people with a new perspective in life.

"What is that in your hand?" the Lord had asked Moses long ago.[10] He answered, "A rod." "Go and work with that rod," God

7. Acts 5:15   9. Mark 5:40-42
8. Acts 3:1-10   10. Exodus 4:2-5

said, "and you will be My servant."

If God had asked Dorcas the same question she would have answered, "A needle and thread, Lord." Then He would have shown her that these were precisely the instruments with which she could serve Him.

The life, death and resurrection of Dorcas helped spread the Gospel. Peter could not leave Joppa for a while because he was needed by the people who were inquiring about God.

Dorcas started a movement that spread beyond the borders of her city and country. Indirectly she became a great evangelist. Today there are Dorcas Groups all over the world. Millions of needy people are fed and clothed by this society.

Who can number the countless women who were influenced by the life of this woman, Dorcas? Her bright example will never be extinguished. That is the most any disciple can desire.

Dorcas, a woman who loved God
(Acts 9:36-42; Romans 12:4-8; James 1:27)

Questions:
1. What was typical of Dorcas' life according to Acts 9:36?
2. Study her dedication in light of Matthew 25:14-29 and Romans 12:4-8 and list your findings.
3. What might have been the background of Dorcas' dedication toward the widows? (Deuteronomy 10:17,18; 14:29)
4. Tell briefly what happened to Dorcas.
5. What do you consider to be the most important result of her resurrection?
6. Which facts in this story appeal to you the most? How will they change your life?

*"No, dear brothers, I am still not all I should
be but I am bringing all my energies to bear
on this one thing: Forgetting the past and looking forward
to what lies ahead, I strain to reach the end
of the race and receive the prize . . ."* Paul*

Lydia,
a businesswoman who gave God first place

Acts 16:11-15,40 Therefore putting out to sea from Troas, we ran a straight course to Samothrace, and on the day following to Neapolis; and from there to Philippi, which is a leading city of the district of Macedonia, a Roman colony; and we were staying in this city for some days. And on the Sabbath day we went outside the gate to a riverside, where we were supposing that there would be a place of prayer; and we sat down and began speaking to the women who had assembled. And a certain woman named Lydia, from the city of Thyatira, a seller of purple fabrics, a worshipper of God, was listening; and the Lord opened her heart to respond to the things spoken by Paul. And when she and her household had been baptized, she urged us, saying, "If you have judged me to be faithful to the Lord, come into my house and stay." And she prevailed upon us . . . .

And they went out of the prison and entered the house of Lydia, and when they saw the brethren, they encouraged them and departed.

*Philippians 3:13,14. Taylor, Kenneth N. *The Living Bible,*
© 1971, Tyndale House Publishers, Wheaton, Illinois.

The Sabbath had started in Philippi.

Philippi was an important city in Macedonia, a center of commerce between the Aegean and Adriatic Seas. This key location was the bridge which connected the Middle East to Europe by means of the Roman highway—the Via Egnatia.

An Asiatic woman walked quickly out of the city to a spot at the river where a prayer meeting would be held. The woman Lydia— the Lydian—was an important person. She directed her own business. She imported purple, a very costly cloth which was worn only by the rich and kings, from her hometown of Thyatira in Asia Minor.

Lydia was well respected. She lived in a spacious house with many servants. It is no wonder she was a successful businesswoman, since the Lydian purple market was renowned in the Graeco-Roman world. Its products were eagerly sought everywhere. Lydia was an intelligent woman, a clear thinker who did her work with enthusiasm and purpose of mind. Her work gave her much contact with interesting people. And being an independent woman, especially in this historical period, was an exceptionally interesting occupation.

She did not, like many business people, become totally engrossed in her work. In spite of her many obligations, she found time for things of greater importance. She wasn't satisfied, as many of her fellow citizens were, with worshipping Apollo. She worshipped the only true God. She took time out for Him in her busy schedule. Lydia realized that as a businesswoman she needed His guidance, which was why she was on her way to this prayer meeting.

The meeting today was very small and for women only. Apparently there were not ten Jewish men in Philippi as were required for a synagogue, so instead the women held an open air meeting. Today some unexpected guests visited the meeting— learned men. Paul, the great evangelist and missionary apostle, and his companions Silas, Luke and Timothy had arrived in the city from Troas.

Initially, Paul had had a different plan. He had wanted to go to Bithynia, but the Spirit of Jesus had prevented him in a vision one night. It had been made clear to him that it was very urgent for him to go to Macedonia.[1] So here he was in Philippi to address these women.

He spoke about the God of Abraham who had sent His Son to this earth to redeem the people, to bridge the gap which sin had created between God and man. He told them that by faith in Jesus Christ, there was redemption, eternal life and a new perspective on living.[2] Lydia listened carefully, with all her heart.

Pascal has said that God created a God-shaped vacuum in the human heart that can only be satisfied by God Himself. Lydia was open to the things of God because her heart craved this deeper experience of faith. Lydia's knowledge of God was superficial. She did not know Him as her Father in Jesus Christ. He could reach her heart easily, however, because it was *King Solomon warned about the importance of keeping watch over the heart in Proverbs 4:23, "Keep your heart with all vigilance; for from it flow the springs of life."* already set on Him and she was sensitive to His Word. It was necessary for her to pay attention to His Word, for while God makes one step toward a person, He then expects the individual to make the next step. God then proves Himself by making the next step.

The seed of the Word fell into her heart as if onto prepared ground,[3] and resulted in a new birth.[4] She found the link that had been missing in her experience—personal faith in Jesus Christ. Lydia had become a Christian. For this energetic woman it meant that she needed to testify openly about it immediately. She wanted everyone to know of the unspeakable happiness that was now within her. She was baptized. By this she said without words, "I identify myself with the death and resurrection of Jesus Christ,[5] and I am going to begin a new life."

This new convert drew others to Christ like a magnet. And who should be the first to hear but her own household. They listened to the Word and also believed. They also confirmed their faith by baptism—and the first church in Philippi was born.

For Paul, there was no longer any question as to why he had been directed to Macedonia. People were being born again. They were the first Christians in Europe. A new continent was opening for the Gospel—through Lydia.

In ages to come an innumerable throng would follow her

1. Acts 16:7-10
2. Acts 3:13-16; Romans 8:1,16,17
3. Luke 8:15
4. I Peter 1:23
5. Romans 6:3-5

example. Like her, they would receive Christ and multiply in following generations. Lydia's enthusiasm for God bore fruit in others' lives. The number of Christians increased through her. This is what God expects all Christians to do. In creation He commanded men and beasts to multiply themselves biologically to fill the earth. They were to bear fruit after their kind.[6] When Jesus talked to His disciples about fruit-bearing,[7] He was speaking of people who could spiritually come to life through the seed of His Word.[8] A Christian can multiply himself spiritually by bringing others to Christ. Lydia did this.

Being a Christian was a very practical matter for Lydia. She did not become a nun, nor even a full-time evangelist. She remained in her occupation. She brought credit to her name by submitting herself, her business and her possessions to maximum service for Christ.

The first thing she submitted was her home. She urged Paul and his companions to stay there. Their acceptance proved they took her faith seriously. In this way she also identified herself with the Gospel to the non-believers. She was not ashamed of Christ. She was not ashamed even when Paul and Silas, bruised and wounded, returned from prison, where they had been taken illegally. Everyone in the city knew that the distinguished Lydia considered it a privilege to lodge these men.

God desires that Christians open their homes to others and serve one another with what they have received from Him. He desires that they be good managers of the material possessions He has entrusted to them.[9] Those who are hospitable will realize later, to their amazement, that sometimes, unknown to them, they have given room to angels.[10] Abraham experienced this.[11] Lydia understood this also, though it was not stated in so many words.

From then on Lydia's earnings would not be an end in themselves, but a means to further the Gospel. Lydia would sell purple to the honor of God. He was at the top of her list of priorities. She was not only in a key position socially but also geographically. The news spread quickly from this commercial city situated on several international travel routes. From then on not only would bags of purple leave Lydia's home, but the Gospel too would travel throughout the civilized world.

6. Genesis 1:24-29

7. John 15:1-16

8. John 17:20

9. I Peter 4:9,10

10. Hebrews 13:2

11. Genesis 18:1-15; 19:1

It is reasonable to assume that a woman who could impress the apostles and her household with her newly founded convictions would be no less successful in convincing her business contacts. Thus, her business was a two-fold success.

Some years later when Paul wrote the Philippian church from his Roman prison, he mentioned the women who worked hard with him to help spread the Gospel.[12] He was probably thinking of Lydia and others he met in her home.

Lydia had been given much and she used it for the Lord. She is touching proof of how much God can do through a person who has made Him the first priority in life.

Lydia, a businesswoman who gave God first place
(Acts 16:11-15,40)

Questions:

1. Where does Lydia appear for the first time and what do you learn of her?
2. What happened when she heard Paul speak? What did God do to her and what did she do herself? (Also see Proverbs 4:23 and Luke 8:15.)
3. After she heard Paul speak, what was her public confession of faith? What can be the only explanation for that?
4. John 15:1-16 talks about bearing fruit. In what ways did Lydia's life bear fruit in the lives of others?
5. Explain which two groups of people she became an instrument for in the ministry of the Gospel. (Also read John 17:20 and I Peter 4:9,10.)
6. How did Lydia prove that she gave first priority to things of God? What did you learn from her and how can you work this out in your life daily?

12. Philippians 1:3-7; 4:3

*"The Coemeterium Priscilla, one of the oldest catacombs
in Rome, and the Titulus Priscilla, a church at the
Aventine in Rome, remind people of the twentieth century
of a woman living at the beginning of this era, whom
Tertullianus called, 'the holy Prisca, who preached the Gospel.'"*
The author

Priscilla,
a valued co-worker in preaching the Gospel

Acts 18:1-4 After these things he left Athens and went to Corinth. And he found a certain Jew named Aquila, a native of Pontus, having recently come from Italy with his wife Priscilla, because Claudius had commanded all the Jews to leave Rome. He came to them, and because he was of the same trade, he stayed with them and they were working; for by trade they were tentmakers. And he was reasoning in the synagogue every Sabbath and trying to persuade Jews and Greeks.

Acts 18:18-20 And Paul, having remained many days longer, took leave of the brethren and put out to sea for Syria, and with him were Priscilla and Aquila. In Cenchrea he had his hair cut, for he was keeping a vow. And they came to Ephesus, and he left them there. Now he himself entered the synagogue and reasoned with the Jews. And when they asked him to stay for a longer time, he did not consent.

Acts 18:24-26 Now a certain Jew named Apollos, an Alexandrian by birth, an eloquent man, came to Ephesus; and he was mighty in the Scriptures. This man had been instructed in the way of the Lord; and being fervent in spirit, he was speaking and teaching accurately the things concerning Jesus, being acquainted only with the baptism of John; and he began to speak out boldly in the synagogue. But when Priscilla and Aquila heard him, they took him aside and explained to him the way of God more accurately.

Romans 16:3-5 Greet Prisca and Aquila, my fellow-workers in Christ Jesus, who for my life risked their own necks, to whom not only do I give thanks, but also all the churches of the Gentiles; also greet the church that is in their house. Greet Epaenetus, my beloved, who is the first convert to Christ from Asia.

I Corinthians 16:19 The churches of Asia greet you. Aquila and Prisca greet you heartily in the Lord, with the church that is in their house.

Priscilla. The fact that her name has been preserved in history is proof that she was a remarkable and distinguished woman. The appearance of her name before her husband's is even further proof of this. However respected and interesting her life in Rome might have been, it came to an abrupt end in A.D. 50 when the emperor Claudius expelled all Jews from that city.

Priscilla and Aquila left Rome and headed back toward Asia Minor where they were born, finally settling in Corinth.

It appeared as if their lives had reached a dead end, but God's blueprint for them would soon reveal an exciting new beginning. A fascinating new life of service was awaiting them.

They had left much behind—their possessions—their friends. But they were a harmonious couple and their marriage was still intact. They had no need of the warning which Paul later made to the loose-living Corinthians when he wrote, "Do not be bound together with unbelievers. For what partnership have righteousness and lawlessness, or what fellowship has light with darkness?"[1]

This couple had become one in a special way, as they walked together in their faith.[2]

They had arrived in Corinth just before Paul. He had confidence in this couple and was willing to invest his life in them in order that the Gospel could be spread further.

1. II Corinthians 6:14
2. Amos 3:3

Both Priscilla and Aquila had learned an occupation. Even rich Jews saw to it that their children learned a trade. A wise saying which supported this practice was, "He that doesn't see to it that his son learns a trade teaches him to be a thief." And hadn't Jesus of Nazareth, the carpenter, indeed proved that working with one's hands was an honorable thing?

They were tentmakers and this trade proved to be a link between them and Paul, for he was also a tentmaker. They not only worked together, they also lived together. Paul well knew that the best kind of training he could give came from being together day after day. Like Jesus, he selected his future co-workers carefully.[3]

They worked in a small outdoor shop, similar to the ones common in the Middle East today. They talked much as, day after day, goatskins and hides changed under their fingers into useful tent coverings. Each day Paul tailored the Word of God to their needs. And they learned how to apply it.[4]

Priscilla and her husband listened eagerly to Paul's teachings. They were interested in the message which Paul preached at the synagogue on the Sabbath. They prayed for him. And when he experienced problems, they were with him, prepared to give their lives for him. Priscilla and Aquila were not only united by their faith and the same trade, but also in their respect and friendship for Paul. This loyalty must have meant much to this lonely man, for shortly before his death, he sent them his greetings.[5]

Priscilla, who watched the smallest details of Paul's life, was as much impressed by what he did as by what he said. A desire was awakened in her to become a follower of this man. He made it very clear how one could follow Christ.[6]

Being orthodox Jews, they knew the Old Testament teachings well. But the new knowledge of a faith in Christ and the working of an indwelling Holy Spirit in the human heart were truths that gave them new dimensions in living.

Paul left Corinth after eighteen months, during which a church had been formed.

Priscilla and Aquila accompanied him to Ephesus. Though the believing Jews there fervently desired him to stay, he left shortly after his arrival. He was on the move again—this time to Caesarea.

The fruit of the time Paul had spent with Priscilla and Aquila

---

3. Mark 3:14   5. II Timothy 4:19
4. Philippians 4:9   6. I Corinthians 11:1

now became evident. He was no longer needed in Ephesus because they could stay there and capably replace him. His life work was being continued through them.

This became very clear when Apollos, a gifted Jewish preacher from Alexandria, arrived in Ephesus. He spoke to the people about Jesus with glowing and convincing words. What he preached was true, but incomplete. Priscilla and Aquila immediately detected where his message fell short. They realized that his preaching stopped with the work of John the Baptist. He didn't know the wonderful Gospel story—the results of the death and resurrection of Christ. He seemed to have never heard about the outpouring of the Holy Spirit.

Showing no condescension, they tactfully invited him into their home where, very personally, they explained the full Gospel to him. The Bible describes this in just a few words, but the part and character of Priscilla cannot be hidden.

She did not hold back because she was a woman, but spoke with such love and tact that the learned and gifted preacher eagerly accepted the words of the lay couple. That was the striking thing about Priscilla, she kept her strong personality in rein as she offered her leadership indirectly.

Was this why the men with whom she co-labored appreciated her? What did Apollos hear from Priscilla and her husband? Precisely what Paul had told them. They proved to Apollos by the Scriptures that Jesus was the promised Messiah, the Christ.

Priscilla and Aquila had started a spiritual chain reaction similar to the one Paul later wrote about to Timothy, his spiritual son, "And the things which you have heard from me in the presence of many witnesses, these entrust to faithful men who will be able to teach others also."[7]

What Paul had taught Priscilla—or Prisca as he liked to call her—and Aquila, they had in turn passed on to Apollos. He also began passing it on to others—to the people of Corinth! Thus, Priscilla and Aquila multiplied themselves. They began to bear spiritual fruit. They touched a life and that life blossomed into a disciple,[8] who they knew they could trust to preach the true and complete Gospel to others also. So while Paul traveled to Palestine before returning to Asia Minor, and while Priscilla and Aquila

7. II Timothy 2:2
8. I Corinthians 16:12

opened their home in Ephesus to build the church, Apollos fed the Christians in Corinth. God's Word grew rapidly because the seed of the Word[9] fell into prepared ground. Personal follow-up caused growth and new life.

After some time the couple was no longer needed in Ephesus. A church had been established there which could continue their work. God called them back to Rome. Claudius was dead. Once again the home of Priscilla and Aquila became the meeting place for Christians, this time in Rome.

Paul now called them his fellow-workers in Jesus Christ. The former pupils had grown into valued co-laborers. They were remembered gratefully in all the churches by the Jews and non-Jews alike.

Their stay in Rome was short, probably because of the gruesome persecution of Christians under Nero. But they were there long enough to begin another church. Wherever they went lives were changed and renewed as people came to believe in Jesus Christ.

They returned to Ephesus. Tradition has it that Priscilla and Aquila finally died as martyrs—beheaded! The Roman Catholic Church commemorates their names on July 8 in the history of the martyrs.

Priscilla was a remarkable woman and wife. Most likely she excelled her husband, since history and inscriptions have mentioned her name and not his. She received a prominent place in history because of her friendship and co-laborship with Paul.

Was she more famous than her husband because she was more intelligent, better educated or stronger of character? Or was she perhaps a Christian before him? Perhaps she led him to Christ?[10] The Bible doesn't say.

Her marriage is fascinating, however. These partners functioned harmoniously together in all aspects of life—in their faith, in their social and spiritual interests, in their friendships, in the place God's Word played in their lives, both for their personal study and preaching and in their willingness to give themselves to others without restriction. Their purpose in life was to give themselves totally to God.

Life requested much from Priscilla. She had to have great vitality to adapt again and again to new situations. She made long

9. I Peter 1:23
10. I Peter 3:1,2

and tiring trips. She risked her life to further the Gospel. She was exceptional for that period of history because she worked with men as an equal, yet won their love and respect.

She did not succumb to the temptation to become the dominating figure in her marriage. She honored the relationship that God desires to see between Himself and the marriage partners.[11]

Ages after her death, her life reveals to women today the secrets of a fruitful life and of a marriage that is useful in proclaiming the Gospel.

Priscilla's life also indicates possibilities which have long been neglected—opening one's home for both evangelism and building of the church. Did Paul learn this from Priscilla and Aquila? For he used this very means in the future, when all other doors had been closed to him.[12] Even today Priscilla inspires many to make their home available for the expansion of the Kingdom of God.

Much more important than Priscilla's name in history is the fact that through the ages she has stimulated people to follow Christ— in more than one way.

Priscilla, a valued co-worker in preaching the Gospel
(Acts 18:1-4, 18-20, 24-26; Romans 16:3-5; I Corinthians 16:19)

Questions:
1. List all the churches in which Priscilla and her husband served. What does this reveal about her character?
2. Compare Priscilla's dedication to the Gospel with Acts 28:30, 31. What proved to be a unique opportunity to further the Gospel?

11. I Corinthians 11:3
12. Acts 28:30,31

3. Study her meeting with Apollos in light of II Timothy 2:2 and list your conclusions.
4. Read Acts 18:24-26 carefully. What conditions had Priscilla met in order to be of service in that situation?
5. Summarize all the opportunities Priscilla utilized to be a useful instrument in the preaching of the Gospel.
6. In which way is she an encouragement or stimulus to you? What are you going to do to follow her example?

If you enjoyed **Her Name Is Woman . . .**
Design for Discipleship is for you.

Design for Discipleship is for the person who wants to become a Christ-centered disciple—who does not accept everything he hears, but wants to know what God says in His Word.

Scripture often discusses the same subject in more than one passage. The *Design for Discipleship* series draws these major teachings on a subject together and then asks penetrating questions to aid in understanding.

Design for Discipleship is not designed to provide just an intellectual understanding of the Scriptures—it is designed to change lives. Application questions scattered throughout each chapter demonstrate how to apply God's Word. By the time a person finishes the seven books in the series, he will be able to draw personal applications from any portion of Scripture and will be on his way to becoming a Christ-centered disciple.

INSIGHT. INFLUENCE.
CHALLENGING YOU TO CHANGE.

Her Name is Woman Book 2

Continuing the practical, insightful discoveries from the best-selling first volume of *Her Name Is Woman*, Gien Karssen adds the stories of twenty-five more women from the pages of Scripture in *Her Name Is Woman, Book 2.*

Her Name Is Woman, Book 2
(Gien Karssen) $11

Becoming a Woman of Influence

Do you seek to have a lasting impact on others? Carol Kent helps you understand principles for building solid relationships through seven simple steps Jesus used to mentor His disciples.
Learn to influence others Jesus' way.

Becoming a Woman of Influence
(Carol Kent) $12

Get your copies today at your local bookstore, through our website, or by calling (800) 366-7788.
Ask for offer **#6024** or a FREE catalog of NavPress resources.

NAVPRESS

BRINGING TRUTH TO LIFE
www.navpress.com

Prices subject to change.